SCANDINAVIAN

classic

BAKING

PAT SINCLAIR

SCANDINAVIAN *classic* BAKING

Photography by Joel Butkowski

PELICAN PUBLISHING COMPANY
GRETNA 2011

The word "Pelican" and the depiction of a pelican are trademarks of Pelican Publishing Company, Inc., and are registered in the U.S. Patent and Trademark Office.

ISBN: 9781589808973
Recipes and Text by Pat Sinclair
Photography by Joel Butkowski
Design and Production by Sea Script Company

Layout based on a design by Kit Wohl

Printed in China

Published by Pelican Publishing Company, Inc.
1000 Burmaster Street, Gretna, Louisiana 70053

Endsheet photographs by Human Spectra / Stockholm Visitors
Board (front) and Terje Rakke / Innovation Norway (back)

To my husband Duncan
and to my family,
who encourage me to try
and support me in every way.
I couldn't do it without you.

CONTENTS

COFFEE BREADS

CAKES

COOKIES

TARTS, FRUIT DESSERTS & PASTRIES

TRADITIONAL FAVORITES

INTRODUCTION

Shortly after my husband and I moved our family to Minnesota over 30 years ago, our church had a fundraising craft fair. In addition to crafts, the kitchen manager offered to make lefse and krumkake for the bake sale as long as someone helped her. I jumped at the chance to learn about these Scandinavian favorites. Although I don't have a lefse griddle, I did purchase a krumkake iron and for many years have included these delicate cookies in family Christmas celebrations. This was my introduction to Scandinavian baking and centuries-old traditions.

There are many people of Scandinavian descent living in Minnesota today because the cool climate and crystal clear lakes are similar to that of Sweden, Norway, Denmark and Finland. Thousands of immigrants crossed the ocean in the 19th century seeking a more prosperous life. Traditional foods, such as lefse, can always be purchased at local supermarkets and krumkake and Julekake appear in bakeries during the holidays.

Working on several local community cookbooks, including *75 and Still Cooking*, a celebration of 75 years for Lutheran Brotherhood, broadened my knowledge of Scandinavian baking and I'm delighted to be sharing it. Some recipes, such as Desert Sand Cookies, are simple and easy and others, such as Princess Cake, take dedication and time but produce rewarding results. Spend a little time baking and share it with someone you love.

SCANDINAVIA: LAND OF THE MIDNIGHT SUN

Scandinavia is the northernmost landmass in Europe and includes Sweden, Norway, Denmark and Finland. It is a land of extreme contrasts, long cold dark winters and summer days when daylight can last for 19 hours. Geographically, it is a land of rolling countryside, dense forests, jagged mountain peaks and rivers, lakes and fjords. Because most of the countries in Scandinavia are surrounded by water, seafood is the backbone of all of their cuisines. The extremes of climate and geography are the reason why hearty stews and meats paired with rustic breads are very popular.

SWEDEN

Sweden is the largest country in Scandinavia, stretching almost 1,000 miles from the Arctic to its southern tip, with a population of approximately 25 million people. Swedish design and architecture are internationally recognized for their clean lines and use of natural materials while preserving the pristine environment. Social democratic ideals and urban planning govern society.

Fruits—such as blueberries, blackberries and lingonberries—combined with rich dairy products, result in luscious pastries and desserts. Holidays in the dark days of winter are filled with light and traditional foods add to the celebration.

NORWAY

Bordered by the North Sea and the Barents Sea, Norway lies along the western edge of the Scandinavian peninsula and features a backbone of mountains running down its center. With sharp mountain peaks and dramatic fjords penetrating into the country along its western and southern edges, Norway is a popular tourist destination.

Stureplan Spa in Sturegallerian
Preben Kristensen / Stockholm Visitors Board

9

The long coastline provides seafood of all kinds and Norways's lakes and fjords are teeming with fish, especially salmon. Due to the climate, Norwegians regard food as fuel and start the day with a hearty breakfast including coffee, breads, meat and cheese.

The discovery of oil in the North Sea has made Norway one of the most prosperous countries in Europe.

DENMARK

Denmark is the second largest country in Scandinavia with a population of over five and a half million. The country sits on a large peninsula and includes several large islands and almost 450 smaller islands. Denmark's government is a constitutional monarchy and the oldest kingdom in Europe. In the past, Denmark had mostly an agricultural economy, but industrialization has created a population shift to cities.

Danish cuisine is hearty and rich and the Danes eat more meat than their neighbors. Smorrobrod, Danish open-faced sandwiches, are recognized around the world and include hundreds of combinations. Danish farms produce pork and pork products and dairy farms provide butter and milk products prized for their richness.

FINLAND

Norway, Sweden, and Russia share borders with Finland and have had an effect on Finnish culture and cuisine. Sweden ruled Finland for more that 600 years while Russian Czars ruled for 100 years. One of the most sparsely populated countries in Europe, Finland became independent in 1917 after the Russian Revolution.

Although one third of its land lies above the Arctic Circle, the Gulf Stream moderates summer temperatures. During cold months, gratins and stews are popular and served with flatbreads and crispbreads. Lingonberries and cloudberries are locally grown fruits. Lapland, the northern part of the country, has influenced the cuisine with reindeer stew, fresh salmon and even bear.

—*Pat Sinclair*

Ice Chapel
VisitFinland.com

SCANDINAVIAN COFFEE BREADS

IN SCANDINAVIA, almost every occasion is celebrated around a "coffee table" containing yeast breads, buttery cookies and delectable cakes. Gatherings recognizing baptisms, confirmations, engagements, anniversaries and birthdays center on this feast of coffee and treats.

Coffee tables can be held any time of the day but usually occur late in the afternoon or early evening and feature at least three courses. The most elaborate have seven or more baked goods ranging from simple fare, like Cardamom Buns, to open-face sandwiches on thin slices of Scandinavian Rye Bread. Cakes, cookies and tarts make up the final course. Each Scandinavian country has a favorite—Lefse, the traditional potato pancake, is a favorite in Norway, Smorrobrod or "open faced" sandwiches in Denmark, Pulla Braid bread in Finland, Cinnamon Buns and Ginger Cookies in Sweden—but the main beverage is always coffee, often "improved" with vodka or aquavit.

Ideally the hostess provides enough plates that guests may take a clean plate each time they return to the table. Today's hostess may purchase the desserts and cakes at a favorite bakery, but coffee and conversation are still the main event.

Midsummer Festival
Yanan Li / Stockholm Visitors Board

Pulla Braid

Because Scandinavians love to offer guests a warm welcome of coffee and coffee breads, bread recipes often produce several loaves. Bread freezes well when it is tightly wrapped, but your friends or relatives would probably be delighted to receive a fresh loaf of homemade bread.

MAKES 3 LOAVES

1 1/2 cups	2% milk		1/2 cup	warm water
3/4 cup	sugar			(105° to 115° F.)
1/2 cup	butter		8 to 8 1/2 cups	all-purpose flour
1 1/2 teaspoons	salt		2	large eggs
1 (1/4 ounce) pkg	active dry yeast		1	large egg, beaten
				Swedish pearl sugar, if desired

Combine milk, sugar, butter and salt in a medium saucepan and heat until bubbles form on the sides of the pan, about 2 to 3 minutes. Cool to 115° F. The butter doesn't have to melt. Pour into the bowl of a heavy-duty mixer. Sprinkle the yeast over the warm water and let stand 5 minutes until the yeast is dissolved.

Add the yeast and stir in 3 cups flour. Beat on medium speed for 3 minutes. Add 2 eggs and beat until blended. By hand, stir in 5 cups flour or enough to make a soft dough.

To knead with a heavy-duty mixer, attach a dough hook and follow the manufacturer's directions.

Place the dough on a well-floured surface and shape it roughly into a ball. Place your fingers on top, curled slightly over the ball, and pull the dough toward you. Then push the dough away, using the heels of your hands. Turn the dough a quarter turn and repeat.

When you begin kneading, the dough will be sticky. Add the remaining flour, a little at a time, as needed. Knead the dough 8 to 10 minutes until it is smooth and elastic.

To judge whether the dough has been sufficiently kneaded, place the dough on the work surface, pull both ends gently, and release. The dough should be smooth and elastic, spring back and no longer be sticky.

Spray a bowl with nonstick cooking spray. Shape the dough into a ball by pulling the sides underneath forming a smooth surface. Place the dough, smooth side down, in the bowl. Turn the dough over, coating it with a little oil. Cover loosely with plastic wrap.

Let the dough rise in a warm place until it doubles in size, about 1 hour. When the dough has doubled, an imprint will remain when you poke two fingers into it.

Line 2 baking sheets with parchment paper or lightly grease. Punch the dough down, releasing excess gas. Place the dough on a lightly floured surface and cut into thirds. Divide 1/3 into 3 pieces and roll each piece into a 16" rope. If the dough becomes difficult to shape, cover and let stand 5 to 10 minutes to relax the gluten.

Place one end of each rope together on a lightly floured surface. Braid loosely, pinching both ends to seal. Fold the sealed ends under and place the braid on a baking sheet. Repeat 2 more times. Loosely cover baking sheets with plastic wrap.

Let the dough rise in a warm place until doubled, about 30 minutes. Test by pressing the dough lightly. If your finger leaves only a slight imprint, the dough is ready. It usually takes about half

The Hanseatic Wharf in Bergen
Andrea Giubelli / Innovation Norway

BAKING WITH YEAST

The most important step in baking yeast breads is using the proper temperature of water to activate the yeast. Because yeast is a living organism, it is easily killed by excess heat. When adding yeast directly to warm water, the water temperature should be between 105° and 115° F. Use a thermometer to measure the water temperature to insure that the yeast is not killed.

Another way to test warm tap water is by sprinkling a few drops on the inside of your wrist. If it feels warm to you, it is a perfect temperature for yeast. Adding warm water to yeast is called "proofing" because the yeast will begin to grow and produce gas "proving" that the yeast is alive. After opening yeast, store any remaining in the refrigerator and use by the date indicated on the package.

the time for the second rise as for the first.

Heat the oven to 375° F. Mix the beaten egg with 1 tablespoon water and brush the loaves. Sprinkle with pearl sugar. Bake 35 to 45 minutes or until deep golden brown and loaf sounds hollow when thumped. Using an instant-read thermometer, measure the temperature in the middle of one loaf. It should read 185° F or higher.

Cool the loaves 10 minutes on a wire cooling rack. Remove from the baking sheets and continue cooling. Allow loaves to cool about 30 minutes before slicing.

Swedish Limpa

Popular during the holidays, limpa bread is moist and hearty, lightly sweetened with molasses and enriched with orange peel, anise seed and/or fennel seed. Most rye breads in Scandinavia are slightly sour, but Swedes prefer it slightly sweet. Serve with butter and jam or preserves or with thin slices of meat and cheese.

Makes 2 loaves

1/4 cup	firmly packed light brown sugar	2 1/2 cups	rye flour
1/4 cup	dark molasses	4 1/2 to 5 cups	all-purpose flour
1 1/2 teaspoons	coarse salt	1 to 2 tablespoons	grated orange rind (rind of 1 orange)
1 1/2 cups	hot water	1 teaspoon	anise seed or fennel seed
3 tablespoons	vegetable shortening	1 tablespoon	cornmeal, if desired
1 (1/4 ounce) pkg	active dry yeast		
1/4 cup	warm water (105° to 115° F.)		

Mix the brown sugar, molasses, salt, hot tap water and shortening in the bowl of a heavy-duty mixer. (You can use tap water that feels hot to the touch but not hot enough to cause burns.) If necessary, cool to 115° F. The shortening doesn't have to melt. Sprinkle the yeast over the warm water and let stand 5 minutes until the yeast is dissolved.

Add the yeast to the mixing bowl. Stir in the rye flour and 2 cups all-purpose flour.

Beat on medium speed for 3 minutes. By hand, stir in 2 1/2 cups all-purpose flour or enough to make a soft dough. Stir in orange rind and anise seed or fennel seed. Because the rye flour doesn't absorb water the same as wheat flour, the dough will remain a little tacky. Be careful not to add too much flour or the bread will be dry.

To knead with a heavy-duty mixer, attach a dough hook and follow the manufacturer's directions.

Place the dough on a well-floured surface and shape it roughly into a ball. Place your fingers on top, curled slightly over the ball, and pull the dough toward you. Then push the dough away, using the heels of your hands. Turn the dough a quarter turn and repeat.

When you begin kneading, the dough will be sticky. Add the remaining flour, a little at a time, if needed. Knead the dough 8 to 10 minutes until it is smooth and elastic.

To judge whether the dough has been sufficiently kneaded, place the dough on the work surface, pull both ends gently, and release. The dough should be smooth and elastic, spring back and no longer be sticky.

Spray a bowl with nonstick cooking spray. Shape the dough into a ball by pulling the sides underneath forming a smooth surface. Place the dough, smooth side down, in the bowl. Turn the dough over, coating it with a little oil. Cover loosely with plastic wrap.

Let the dough rise in a warm place until it doubles in size, 1 to 1 1/2 hours. When the dough has doubled, an imprint will remain when you poke two fingers into it.

Lightly grease a baking sheet and sprinkle with cornmeal. Punch the dough down, and place it on a lightly floured surface. Cut the dough in half.

Skating to School
Henrik Trygg / Stockholm Visitors Board

RYE FLOUR

Rye grows in cool climates on poor soil and is used in many "peasant" style breads. Flour made from rye is higher in thiamine, iron, phosphorous and potassium than wheat flour, but is low in gluten. Because of its low gluten content, it is important to use rye flour in combination with wheat flour. Rye flour is available in most supermarkets today, although you may need to look in the natural foods sections.

Shape each half of the dough into a round loaf. Smooth the top of the dough by pulling the sides to the back. If the dough becomes difficult to shape, cover and let stand 5 to 10 minutes to relax the gluten. Place on a baking sheet. Repeat with the second half of the dough. Loosely cover the loaves with plastic wrap.

Let the dough rise in a warm place until doubled, about 45 minutes. Test by pressing the dough lightly. If your finger leaves only a slight imprint, the dough is ready. It usually takes about half the time for the second rise as for the first.

Heat the oven to 375° F. Bake 35 to 45 minutes or until the loaves are a deep golden brown and sound hollow when thumped. Using an instant-read thermometer, measure the temperature in the middle of one loaf. It should read 185° F or higher.

Cool the loaves 5 minutes on a wire cooling rack. Remove the loaves from the baking sheet and continue cooling. Allow the loaves to cool about 30 minutes before slicing.

Norwegian Julekake

Warm from the oven and slathered with butter, Julekake is a holiday tradition in many households. Fresh ground cardamom reflects Scandinavian roots. You can use any variety of candied or dried fruits, but candied citron and raisins are traditional. Use candied green and red cherries that are available in supermarkets around the holidays to add colorful decorations to the loaves, or simply dust generously with confectioners' sugar.

Snow Laden Holly Bush
Marte Kopperud/Innovation Norway

CHRISTMAS CAKE

Julekake translates into "yule" (Christmas) "kake" (cake). A tradition in many Norwegian families, this festive holiday bread made from rich yeast dough is bursting with candied fruits and almonds. Danes also bake similar bread sparkling with candied fruit for holiday events. Swedes add saffron, an expensive and brilliantly colored spice in keeping with the celebrations of the season.

MAKES 2 LOAVES

1 1/2 cups	2% milk		1 cup	candied fruit (citron, cherries, orange peel)
1/2 cup	sugar			
1/2 cup	butter		1/2 cup	slivered almonds, toasted
1 teaspoon	salt			
2 (1/4 ounce) pkgs	active dry yeast		1	large egg, beaten
1/2 cup	warm water (105° to115° F.)		2 cups	confectioners' sugar, sifted
6 to 7 cups	all-purpose flour		4 to 5 tablespoons	heavy whipping cream or milk
1 teaspoon	ground cardamom			
1	large egg		Candied fruit, if desired	
1 cup	golden raisins or raisins			

Combine the milk, sugar, butter and salt in a medium saucepan and heat until small bubbles form on the side of the pan, about 2 to 3 minutes. Cool to 115° F. The butter doesn't have to melt. Pour into the bowl of a heavy-duty mixer. Sprinkle the yeast over the warm water in a small bowl and let stand 5 minutes until the yeast is dissolved.

Add the yeast and stir in 3 cups flour and cardamom. Beat on medium speed for 3 minutes. Beat in the egg. By hand, stir in 3 to 4 cups flour or enough to make a soft dough. Stir in the raisins, candied fruit and almonds.

To knead with a heavy-duty mixer, attach a dough hook and follow the manufacturer's directions.

Place the dough on a well-floured surface and shape it roughly into a ball. Place your fingers on top, curled slightly over the ball, and pull the dough toward you. Then push dough away, using the heels of your hands. Turn dough a quarter turn and repeat.

When you begin kneading, the dough will be sticky. Add the remaining flour, a little at a time, if needed. Knead the dough 8 to 10 minutes until it is smooth and elastic.

Spray a bowl with nonstick cooking spray. Shape the dough into a ball by pulling sides underneath forming a smooth surface. Place the dough, smooth side down, in the bowl. Turn the dough over, coating it with a little oil. Cover loosely with plastic wrap.

Let the dough rise in a warm place until it doubles in size, about 1 hour. When it has doubled, an imprint will remain when you poke two fingers into the dough.

Line a baking sheet with parchment paper or lightly grease. Punch the dough down, and place it on a lightly floured surface. Cut the dough in half.

Shape each half into an oval loaf, about 10" x 4". Pull the sides of the dough to the bottom, smoothing the top. If the dough becomes difficult to shape, cover and let stand 5 to 10 minutes

to relax the gluten. Place on the baking sheet, smooth side up. Repeat with the other portion of dough. Loosely cover with plastic wrap.

Let the dough rise in a warm place until doubled, about 30 minutes. Test by pressing the dough lightly. If your finger leaves only a slight imprint, the dough is ready. It usually takes about half the time for the second rise as for the first.

Heat the oven to 375° F. Mix the beaten egg with 1 tablespoon water and brush the loaves. Bake 35 to 45 minutes or until loaves are deep golden brown and sound hollow when thumped. Using an instant-read thermometer, measure temperature in middle of one loaf. It should read 185° F or higher.

Cool the loaves on a wire cooling rack. Allow the loaves to cool about 30 minutes before slicing when serving warm. Cool completely to spread with confectioners' sugar glaze.

Combine the confectioners' sugar and whipping cream in a medium bowl and beat until smooth. Spread on tops of loaves.

Scandinavian Rye Bread

Brushing the loaves with molasses before baking adds a shiny glaze to the tops. If you only have one loaf pan, shape the second loaf into a ball and place on a greased baking sheet. This is a mild rye bread and delicious as a base for Danish smørrobrod, especially if you use rich Danish butter.

MAKES 2 LOAVES

2 cups	2% milk	1 teaspoon	salt
1/3 cup	firmly packed light brown sugar	1 (1/4 ounce) pkg	active dry yeast
1/2 cup plus 2 tablespoons	dark molasses, divided	1/2 cup	warm water (105° to 115° F.)
		1 1/2 cups	rye flour
1/2 cup	vegetable shortening	6 to 7 cups	all-purpose flour
		1 tablespoon	water

Combine the milk, brown sugar, 1/2 cup molasses, shortening and salt in a medium saucepan and heat until small bubbles form on the side of the pan, about 2 to 3 minutes. Cool to 115° F. The shortening doesn't have to melt. Pour into the bowl of a heavy-duty mixer. Sprinkle the yeast over the warm water and let stand 5 minutes until the yeast is dissolved.

Add the yeast and stir in the rye flour and 3 cups all-purpose flour. Beat on medium speed for 3 minutes. By hand or on low speed, stir in 3 cups all-purpose flour or enough to make a soft dough. Because the dough has rye flour it will remain a little tacky.

To knead with a heavy-duty mixer, attach a dough hook and follow the manufacturer's directions.

Place the dough on a well-floured surface and shape it roughly into a ball. Place your fingers on top, curled slightly over the ball, and pull the dough toward you. Then push the dough away, using the heels of your hands. Turn the dough a quarter turn and repeat.

When you begin kneading, the dough will be sticky. Add remaining flour, a little at a time, if needed. Knead the dough 8 to 10 minutes until it is smooth and elastic.

To judge whether the dough has been sufficiently kneaded, place the dough on the work surface, pull both ends gently, and release. The dough should be smooth and elastic, spring back and no longer be sticky.

Spray a bowl with nonstick cooking spray. Shape the dough into a ball by pulling sides underneath forming a smooth surface. Place the dough, smooth side down, in the bowl. Turn the dough over coating it with a little oil. Cover loosely with plastic wrap.

Let the dough rise in a warm place until it doubles in size, about 1 hour. When it has doubled, an imprint will remain when you poke two fingers into the dough.

Grease two 9" x 5" loaf pans. Punch the dough down, and place it on a lightly floured surface. Cut the dough in half.

Roll out one of the halves to a 14" x 9" rectangle. If the dough becomes difficult to shape, cover and let stand 5 to 10 minutes to relax the gluten. Roll the dough up from the short side and pinch edges to seal. Place in a greased pan with the seam on the bottom, folding ends under. Repeat with the second loaf. Loosely cover loaf pans with plastic wrap.

SMORREBROD

Smørrobrod means "buttered bread" and is the everyday lunch for thousands of Danes in hundreds of combinations.

Let the dough rise in a warm place until doubled, about 30 to 45 minutes. Test by pressing the dough lightly. If your finger leaves only a slight imprint, the dough is ready. It usually takes about half the time for the second rise as for the first.

Heat the oven to 375° F. Combine the remaining 2 tablespoons molasses and 1 tablespoon water and brush on tops of loaves. Using a sharp knife or razor blade, make 3 diagonal slashes on top of each loaf about 1/2" deep.

Bake the loaves 35 to 45 minutes or until dark brown and loaves sound hollow when thumped. Using an instant-read thermometer, measure the temperature in the middle of one loaf. It should read 185° F or higher.

Cool the loaves 5 minutes on a wire cooling rack. Remove loaves from the pans and continue cooling. Cool about 30 minutes before slicing.

Cardamom Breakfast Buns

Swedish pearl sugar can be found in most supermarkets in the baking section or you can sprinkle the buns with granulated sugar. Especially for these buns, I recommend grinding fresh cardamom seeds for their unique flavor. All of the Scandinavian countries have a version of these.

MAKES 12 BUNS

1 cup	2% milk	4 1/2 to 5 cups	all-purpose flour
1/2 cup	sugar	1 teaspoon	ground cardamom
1/4 cup	butter	1/2 cup	raisins
1/4 teaspoon	salt	1	large egg, beaten
1 (1/4 ounce) pkg	active dry yeast	Swedish pearl sugar	
1/4 cup	warm water (105° to 115° F.)		

Combine the milk, sugar, butter and salt in a medium saucepan and heat over medium heat until small bubbles form on the side of the pan, about 2 to 3 minutes. Remove from the heat and cool to 115° F. The butter doesn't need to be melted. Pour into the bowl of a heavy-duty mixer. Sprinkle the yeast over the warm water and let stand 5 minutes until the yeast is dissolved.

Add the yeast and stir in 2 cups flour and cardamom. Beat on medium speed for 3 minutes. Add raisins. By hand, stir in 2 1/2 cups flour or enough to make a soft dough.

To knead with a heavy-duty mixer, attach a dough hook and follow the manufacturer's directions.

Place the dough on a well-floured surface and shape it roughly into a ball. Place your fingers on top, curled slightly over the ball, and pull the dough toward you. Then push the dough away, using the heels of your hands. Turn the dough a quarter turn and repeat.

When you begin kneading, the dough will be sticky. Add remaining flour, a little at a time, if needed. Knead the dough 8 to 10 minutes until it is smooth and elastic.

To judge whether the dough has been sufficiently kneaded, place the dough on the work surface, pull both ends gently and release. The dough should be smooth and elastic, no longer sticky and should spring back.

Spray a bowl with nonstick cooking spray. Shape the dough into a ball by pulling the sides underneath forming a smooth surface. Place the dough, smooth side down, in the bowl. Turn the dough over, coating it with a little oil. Cover loosely with plastic wrap.

Let the dough rise in a warm place until it doubles in size, about 1 hour. When the dough has doubled, the imprint will remain when you poke two fingers into it.

Lightly grease a 13" x 9" baking pan. Punch the dough down and place it on a lightly floured surface. Divide the dough into 12 pieces. Shape the dough into balls by pulling the sides of the dough underneath and smoothing the tops. Place the balls in the prepared pan.

Loosely cover the pans with plastic wrap. Let the dough rise in a warm place until doubled, about 30 minutes. Test by pressing the dough lightly. If your finger leaves only a slight imprint, the dough is ready. It usually takes about half the time for the second rise as for the first.

Landscape near Karrebaeksminde
Cees van Roeden / Danish Media Center

CARDAMOM

Cardamom is a member of the ginger family and is used a great deal in Scandinavian baking. A jar of ground cardamom lacks the depth of flavor found when the seeds are freshly ground. A cardamom pod contains 17 to 20 tiny seeds surrounded by a papery green outer skin that is easily split.

Grinding the seeds in a mortar and pestle releases the fragrant oils. The tiny seeds can also be ground in a coffee grinder. Because the essential oils begin to break down as soon as they are released, the best flavor results from splitting the pods and grinding the seeds just before adding. Cardamom is expensive but the pods stay fresh for a long time when stored in a glass jar away from heat.

Heat the oven to 375° F. Mix the beaten egg with 1 tablespoon water and brush over the buns. Sprinkle with pearl sugar.

Bake 15 to 18 minutes or until golden brown. Cool the buns on a wire cooling rack at least 5 minutes before serving warm or remove from the pan and cool completely.

St. Lucia Buns

Saffron is the most expensive spice in the world because it's harvested by hand. The brilliant color comes from the yellow-orange stigmas of a purple crocus. Using it in buns for St. Lucia's feast day on December 13th highlights the importance of the day.

MAKES 16 BUNS

1 cup	2% milk		1/4 cup	warm water
1/2 cup	sugar			(105° to 115° F.)
1/2 cup	butter		4 1/2 to 5 cups	all-purpose flour
1/2 teaspoon	salt		2	large eggs
1 teaspoon	saffron threads, crushed		32	raisins
1 (1/4 ounce) pkg	active dry yeast		1	large egg, beaten

Combine the milk, sugar, butter and salt in a medium saucepan and heat over medium heat until small bubbles form on the side of the pan, about 2 to 3 minutes. Remove from the heat and add the saffron. Cool to 115° F. The butter doesn't need to be melted. Pour into the bowl of a heavy-duty mixer. Sprinkle the yeast over the warm water and let stand 5 minutes until the yeast is dissolved.

Add the yeast and stir in 2 cups all-purpose flour. Beat on medium speed for 3 minutes. Beat in the eggs. By hand, stir in 2 1/2 cups flour or enough to make a soft dough.

To knead with a heavy-duty mixer, attach a dough hook and follow the manufacturer's directions.

Place the dough on a well-floured surface and shape it roughly into a ball. Place your fingers on top, curled slightly over the ball, and pull the dough toward you. Then push the dough away, using the heels of your hands. Turn the dough a quarter turn and repeat.

When you begin kneading, the dough will be sticky. Add remaining flour, a little at a time, if needed. Knead the dough 8 to 10 minutes until it is smooth and elastic.

To judge whether the dough has been sufficiently kneaded, place the dough on the work surface, pull both ends gently, and release. The dough should be smooth and elastic, spring back and no longer be sticky.

Spray a bowl with nonstick cooking spray. Shape the dough into a ball by pulling sides underneath forming a smooth surface. Place the dough, smooth side down, in the bowl. Turn the dough over, coating it with a little oil. Cover loosely with plastic wrap.

Let the dough rise in a warm place until it doubles in size, about 1 hour. When the dough has doubled, an imprint will remain when you poke two fingers into it.

Line 2 baking sheets with parchment paper or lightly grease. Punch the dough down, and place it on a lightly floured surface. Cut the dough into 16 pieces.

Roll each piece of dough into a 12" rope. Shape a bun by forming an "S" shape and curling ends in opposite directions forming a coil. Place on a prepared baking sheet. Place a raisin in the center of each coil. Cover loosely with plastic wrap.

Let the buns rise in a warm place until doubled, about 30 minutes. Test by pressing the dough lightly. If your finger leaves only a slight imprint, the dough is ready. It usually takes about half the time for the second rise as for the first.

St. Lucia Day Choir
Henrik Trygg/Stockholm Visitors Board

FEAST DAY OF ST. LUCIA

The Christmas season begins in Sweden early in December with the celebration of the Feast of St. Lucia. On the morning of December 13th, the oldest girl in the family portrays St. Lucia. Dressed in white, she wears a crown of candles on her head and brings a special Lucia Day breakfast to her parents' bed. Uniquely shaped yeast buns flavored with saffron, hot coffee and cocoa, and maybe some pepparkakor (ginger cookies) are traditionally served. Her younger sisters also dress in white to help her, but carry only one lit candle. Many towns and churches also have special events to celebrate this holiday.

Heat the oven to 400° F. Brush the buns with beaten egg. Bake 15 to 20 minutes or until deep golden brown.

Cool the buns on a wire cooling rack.

Shrove Tuesday Buns

Semlor, or Shrove Tuesday Buns, were originally served on the day before Ash Wednesday. The richness of these buns is a contrast with the coming lean days of Lent. Use a pastry bag to pipe the whipped cream into the center for a special touch.

MAKES 16 BUNS

3/4 cup	2% milk	4 to 4 1/2 cups	all-purpose flour
1/2 cup	butter	1 teaspoon	baking powder
1/3 cup plus		1	large egg
2 tablespoons	sugar, divided	1	large egg, beaten
1/2 teaspoon	salt	1/2 cup	almond paste
1 (1/4 ounce) pkg	active dry yeast	1 1/4 cups	heavy whipping
1/4 cup	warm water		cream, divided
	(105° to 115° F.)	Confectioners' sugar	

Combine the milk, butter, 1/3 cup sugar and salt in a medium saucepan and heat until small bubbles form on the side of the pan, about 2 to 3 minutes. Cool to 115° F. The butter doesn't need to be melted. Pour into the bowl of a heavy-duty mixer. Sprinkle the yeast over the warm water and let stand 5 minutes until the yeast is dissolved.

Add the yeast and stir in 2 cups flour and the baking powder. Mix with an electric mixer on medium speed for 3 minutes. Beat in the egg. By hand or with the mixer on low speed, add 2 cups flour or enough to make a soft dough.

To knead with a heavy-duty mixer, attach a dough hook and follow the manufacturer's directions.

Place the dough on a well-floured surface and shape it roughly into a ball. Place your fingers on top, curled slightly over the ball, and pull the dough toward you. Then push the dough away using the heels of your hands. Turn the dough a quarter turn and repeat.

When you begin kneading, the dough will be sticky. Add the remaining flour, a little at a time, if needed. Knead the dough 8 to 10 minutes until it is smooth and elastic.

To judge whether the dough has been sufficiently kneaded, place the dough on the work surface, pull both ends gently, and release. The dough should be smooth and elastic, no longer sticky and should spring back.

Spray a bowl with nonstick cooking spray. Shape the dough into a ball by pulling sides underneath forming a smooth surface. Place the dough, smooth side down, in the bowl. Turn the dough over, coating it with a little oil. Cover loosely with plastic wrap.

Let the dough rise in a warm place until it doubles in size, about 45 to 60 minutes. When the dough has doubled, the imprint will remain when you poke two fingers into it.

Line a baking sheet with parchment paper or grease lightly. Punch the dough down, and place on a lightly floured surface. Divide the dough into 16 pieces. Shape each piece into a ball by pulling the sides of dough underneath and smoothing the top. Place the balls on the baking sheet.

Loosely cover with plastic wrap. Let the dough rise in a warm place until doubled, about 30 minutes. Test by pressing the dough lightly. If your finger leaves only a slight imprint, the dough is ready. It usually takes about half the time for the second rise as for the first.

Blossoms and Steeple
Human Spectra / Stockholm Visitors Board

SHROVE TUESDAY

Shrove Tuesday, the day before Ash Wednesday, signals the beginning of the Lenten season. These buns, also known as Semlor, are rich with butter, eggs and cream and eaten as a way of preparing for the Lenten fast. Today they are served from January until Easter. They can be served with coffee or in a bowl of milk for breakfast or as a treat in a bowl of hot chocolate.

Heat the oven to 400° F. Mix the beaten egg with 1 tablespoon water and brush on tops of the buns. Bake 12 to 15 minutes or until golden brown. Cool the buns on a wire cooling rack. When buns are cool, slice horizontally in half using a bread knife or serrated knife.

Mix the almond paste with 1/4 cup whipping cream until softened. (If almond paste is very stiff, grate it or use a food processor to chop it.) Spread 1 rounded teaspoon onto the cut surface of the bottom of each bun.

Whip the remaining whipping cream with electric mixer on high speed until soft peaks form. Scrape down the sides of the bowl. On low speed, beat in the remaining 2 tablespoons of sugar.

Spread whipped cream on top of the almond paste and cover with the top of the buns. Sprinkle with confectioners' sugar. These buns must be kept in the refrigerator.

27

Cinnamon Rolls

Because the yeast isn't added directly to the liquid, the temperature of the liquid can be higher which helps the bread rise a little faster. Make this recipe even simpler by using a heavy-duty mixer with a dough hook to knead the dough.

MAKES 15 ROLLS

3/4 cup	2% milk		1 teaspoon	salt
1/4 cup	water		1	large egg
1/2 cup	butter, softened		2 tablespoons	butter, melted
5 to 5 1/2 cups	all-purpose flour		1 cup	firmly packed
1/2 cup	sugar			light brown sugar
1 (1/4 ounce) pkg	active dry yeast		1 1/2 teaspoons	cinnamon

FROSTING

1 1/2 cups	confectioners' sugar		3 tablespoons	2% milk
3 tablespoons	butter, softened		1/2 teaspoon	almond extract

Heat the milk and water to 120° to 130° F. Add butter. The butter does not need to melt completely.

Combine 2 cups flour, sugar, yeast and salt in the bowl of a heavy-duty mixer. Add the milk mixture and beat on medium speed until mixed. Scrape down the sides of the bowl and beat 3 minutes. Beat in the egg and add enough flour to make a soft dough, about 3 cups.

To knead with a heavy-duty mixer, attach a dough hook and follow the manufacturer's directions.

Place the dough on a well-floured surface and shape it roughly into a ball. Place your fingers on top, curled slightly over the ball, and pull the dough toward you. Then push the dough away, using the heels of your hands. Turn the dough a quarter turn and repeat.

When you begin kneading, the dough will be sticky. Add the remaining flour, a little at a time, if needed. Knead the dough 8 to 10 minutes until it is smooth and elastic.

To judge whether the dough has been sufficiently kneaded, place the dough on the work surface, pull both ends gently, and release. The dough should be smooth and elastic, no longer sticky and should spring back.

Shape the dough into a ball by pulling the sides underneath to form a smooth top. Place it top side down in an oiled bowl. Turn the dough right side up, coating it with a little oil. Cover loosely with plastic wrap.

Let the dough rise in a warm place 1 hour or until it doubles. When the dough has doubled, the imprint will remain when you poke two fingers into it.

Lightly grease a 13" x 9" baking pan.

Punch the dough down and place it on a lightly floured surface. Roll out the dough to a 18" x 9" rectangle. Spread evenly with melted butter and sprinkle with brown sugar and cinnamon. Roll the dough up, starting with the long edge, and pinch edges to seal.

Royal Stockholm
Christer Lundin / Stockholm Visitors Board

LAND OF THE MIDNIGHT SUN

Scandinavia is called the Land of the Midnight Sun because during the summer, the sun never sets at the higher latitudes. In the lower latitudes, summer days are long, sometimes lasting 19 hours, while the nights are short. In the winter, the reverse is true and daylight is scarce. About 25% of Finland lies north of the Artic Circle and the sun doesn't set from May until mid-July during the summer. Although the growing season is short, fruits and vegetables seem to have concentrated flavors from growing in constant light.

Cut into 15 slices (about 1" thick). Place the rolls in a prepared pan. Loosely cover pan with plastic wrap and let rolls rise in a warm place 30 to 40 minutes or until doubled. Test by pressing the dough lightly. A gentle touch should leave no imprint.

Heat the oven to 350° F. Bake 40 to 50 minutes or until the buns are golden brown. Cool slightly.

Combine the confectioners' sugar, butter, milk and almond extract in a medium bowl and beat until smooth. Pour over warm cinnamon buns.

Danish Almond Tea Ring

Danish Tea Ring is filled with almond paste, a combination of ground almonds and sugar. Almond paste can be purchased in the baking aisle of most supermarkets, either in a can or a tube encased in plastic. When possible, press the tubes and select ones that are softer when you press the sides.

MAKES 1 RING, 12 TO 16 SERVINGS

3/4 cup	2% milk		1 teaspoon	almond extract
1/2 cup	sugar		5 to 6 cups	all-purpose flour
1/2 cup	butter		2	large eggs
1 teaspoon	salt		1 (8 ounces) can	almond paste
1 (1/4 ounce) pkg	active dry yeast		2 tablespoons	sugar
1/4 cup	warm water		1	large egg white
	(105° to 115° F.)		1/2 teaspoon	vanilla

FROSTING

1 1/2 cups	confectioners' sugar		2 tablespoons	2% milk
3 tablespoons	butter, softened		1/2 teaspoon	vanilla

Combine the milk, sugar, butter and salt in a medium saucepan and heat until small bubbles form on the sides of the pan, about 2 to 3 minutes. Cool to 115° F. The butter doesn't need to be melted. Pour into the bowl of a heavy-duty mixer. Sprinkle the yeast over the warm water and let stand 5 minutes until the yeast is dissolved.

Add the yeast and almond extract. Stir in 2 cups flour. Mix with electric mixer on medium speed for 3 minutes. Add eggs and beat well. By hand or with a mixer on low speed, add 3 cups flour or enough to make a soft dough.

To knead with a heavy-duty mixer, attach a dough hook and follow the manufacturer's directions.

Place the dough on a well-floured surface and shape it roughly into a ball. Place your fingers on top, curled slightly over the ball, and pull the dough toward you. Then push the dough away, using the heels of your hands. Turn the dough a quarter turn and repeat.

When you begin kneading, the dough will be sticky. Add remaining flour, a little at a time, if needed. Knead the dough 8 to 10 minutes until it is smooth and elastic.

To judge whether the dough has been sufficiently kneaded, place the dough on the work surface, pull both ends gently, and release. The dough should be smooth and elastic, no longer sticky and should spring back.

Spray a bowl with nonstick cooking spray and shape the dough into a ball by pulling the sides underneath forming a smooth surface. Place the dough smooth side down in the bowl. Turn the dough over, coating it with a little oil. Cover loosely with plastic wrap.

Let the dough rise in a warm place until it doubles in size, about 1 to 1 1/2 hours. When the dough has doubled, an imprint will remain when you poke two fingers into it.

Line a baking sheet with parchment paper or grease with shortening. Beat almond paste, sugar, egg white and vanilla in a medium bowl until well mixed. (If almond paste is very stiff, grate it or use a food processor to chop it.)

Half-Timbered House in Faaborg
John Sommer / Danish Media Center

DENMARK

Denmark, the oldest constitutional monarchy in Europe, is a land of contrasts from modern Danish architecture to quaint half-timbered houses.

Punch the dough down, and place on a lightly floured surface. Roll the dough to a 22" x 15" rectangle. Spread filling halfway over the dough, spreading to within 1" along the long side. Starting with the long side, roll up tightly, pressing edge to seal. Place on the baking sheet, seam side down. Shape into a ring and join ends, pinching to seal. Using scissors, make cuts from the outer edge to 1/2" from the inner edge and separate slices slightly. Loosely cover with plastic wrap.

Let the dough rise in a warm place until doubled, about 45 minutes. Test by pressing the dough lightly. If your finger leaves only a slight imprint, the dough is ready. It usually takes about half the time for the second rise as for the first.

Heat the oven to 375 °F. Bake 25 to 30 minutes or until dark golden brown. Cool on a wire cooling rack. Makes the frosting. Mix the confectioners' sugar, 2 tablespoons milk and almond extract until smooth. Drizzle over baked ring. Serve warm or at room temperature.

Rieska Finnish Flatbread

For this bread, I prefer medium ground rye flour because it adds a nutty flavor and chewy texture and is high in nutrients. Brush the loaves with butter after baking and serve with meat and cheese for a casual meal.

MAKES **2** LARGE FLATBREADS, **8** SLICES EACH

3 cups	all-purpose flour		1 teaspoon	salt
1 1/2 cups	rye flour		1/2 cup	vegetable shortening
1/4 cup	sugar		2 cups	lowfat buttermilk
1 tablespoon	baking powder			
1 teaspoon	baking soda			

Heat the oven to 400° F.

Combine flour, rye flour, sugar, baking powder, baking soda and salt in a large mixing bowl. Cut in shortening with a pastry blender until coarse crumbs form.

Stir in the buttermilk and mix until the flour is moistened. (To make a substitute for buttermilk, place 1 tablespoon vinegar or lemon juice for each cup into a measuring cup and add milk to measure 1 cup. Let stand for 5 to 10 minutes before using.)

Place the dough onto a lightly floured surface. Lightly knead the dough 6 to 8 times and shape into a ball.

Divide the dough in half. Pat each half of the dough into an 8" round, about 1/2" thick. Place on a baking sheet and prick generously with a fork.

Bake 20 to 25 minutes or until lightly browned. Cool slightly on a wire cooling rack. Cut into wedges to serve.

Feeding the Reindeer
VisitFinland.com

RIESKA

Although Rieska is a traditional Finnish flatbread, it varies in different parts of the country. Whether it is made of oat, barley or rye flour, it's formed into large flat loaves that can vary in thickness from cracker-thin to thick and bread-like. The rye flour combined with buttermilk in this version adds a slightly sour flavor.

Rye grows in poorer climates and thinner soil than wheat and is probably the reason that it is so popular in Scandinavian countries. It used to be shaped into large rounds with a 2" hole in the center created by punching through with a cow's horn. To store many loaves of bread, a pole was run through the center holes and hung from the rafters to be used over several months.

Blueberry Rhubarb Muffins

Sweet blueberries and tart chunks of rhubarb baked into tender muffins, fragrant with the scent of cinnamon, trumpet the arrival of spring. Because it grows in cooler climates, rhubarb is a popular fruit in Scandinavia. When fresh rhubarb is out of season, you can use frozen rhubarb in this recipe. Don't thaw before adding it, but increase the baking time slightly.

MAKES **12** MUFFINS

Blueberries in Spring
Pekka Luukkola / VisitFinland.com

TOPPING

2 tablespoons	sugar	1 teaspoon	cinnamon
2 tablespoons	all-purpose flour	2 tablespoons	butter

2 cups	all-purpose flour	1 cup	2% milk
1/2 cup	firmly packed light brown sugar	1/3 cup	butter, melted
1 tablespoon	baking powder	1	large egg, beaten
1 teaspoon	cinnamon	1 teaspoon	vanilla
1/4 teaspoon	salt	1/2 cup	blueberries
		1/2 cup	chopped rhubarb

Heat the oven to 400° F. Lightly spray a standard 12-cup muffin pan with nonstick cooking spray or line with paper liners.

In a small bowl, combine the sugar, flour and cinnamon for the topping. Cut in the butter with a pastry blender until mixture resembles coarse crumbs and set aside.

Mix the flour, brown sugar, baking powder, cinnamon and salt in a large bowl.

Combine the milk, butter, egg, and vanilla in a small bowl and add to the flour mixture. Stir only until the flour is moistened. Stir in the blueberries and rhubarb. The batter doesn't need to be smooth.

Divide the batter into the prepared muffin cups, using about 1/4 cup in each. Sprinkle topping mixture over each muffin.

Bake 18 to 23 minutes or until golden brown and a toothpick inserted in the center of a couple of muffins comes out clean. Cool slightly on a wire cooling rack. Run a thin spatula around the edge of each muffin and remove from the pan. Serve warm.

WALPURGIS

Walpurgis, heralding the arrival of spring, is celebrated in Central and Northern Europe with huge bonfires, dancing and music, although spring weather doesn't always appear.

St. Walpurga was an eighth century saint, canonized on May 1st. It's a national holiday in Sweden and Finland, beginning the evening of April 30th and continuing through May 1st. In Sweden, a choral country, singing of traditional songs by choruses is an important part of the celebration. Since the end of the 19th century, the most vibrant and most traditional celebrations involve students and are still found in the university towns such as Uppsala and Lund. These fun celebrations include lots of vodka and beer.

SCANDINAVIAN CAKES

MANY SCANDINAVIAN CAKES are light airy layers spread generously with whipped cream and layered with more whipped cream or custard. Rarely are they topped with frosting but a light dusting with confectioners' sugar is common. Although some cakes contain baking powder, most of the lightness comes from the air that is beaten into egg whites or whole eggs. For cakes that include fat, it is always butter. A cake is always included on a Coffee Table, delicately flavored with vanilla or almond, and usually covered in luscious whipped cream.

When nuts are included, almonds are the most common but sometime hazelnuts, growing wild throughout Europe, add a welcome crunch. Ground almonds are used in almond paste and are also the base for marzipan, a bittersweet confection that is rolled or shaped to use as a decoration. This malleable paste can be lightly colored by kneading with food colors and then rolled out and used to enfold Princess Cakes.

Summertime is berry cake time and light sponge layers with slathered with whipped cream and fresh juicy berries such as Strawberries Cream Cake are a favorite, often eaten outdoors in the warm sunshine

Copenhagen at Dusk
Nicolai Perjesi / Danish Media Center

Lemon Sponge Pudding Cake

A friend in college served me this pudding-like cake when I went to her house to babysit and it instantly became a favorite. It's a combination of a soufflé and a thick creamy sauce, but much easier to make.

MAKES 6 SERVINGS

3	large eggs, separated		1/4 cup	all-purpose flour
1 cup	2% milk		1/8 teaspoon	salt
1/4 cup (2 lemons)	lemon juice		3 tablespoons	butter, melted and cooled
3/4 cup	sugar			Confectioners' sugar

Heat the oven to 350° F.

Generously butter a 1 1/2 quart casserole or 9" x 9" baking dish. Sprinkle with sugar.

Beat the egg yolks in a medium bowl with a whisk until well blended. Stir in the milk and lemon juice.

Combine the sugar, flour and salt in a small bowl and stir into the egg mixture. Beat until smooth. Stir in the butter.

Beat the egg whites with an electric mixer on high speed until soft peaks form. Gently fold into the pudding, retaining as much air as possible. Pour into the prepared baking dish.

Place the dish in a 13" x 9" baking dish and add boiling water to a depth of about 1" around the casserole.

Bake 30 to 40 minutes or until puffed and lightly browned. Carefully remove the casserole from the 9" x 13" dish. Cool slightly before serving. Dust with a little confectioners' sugar. Pudding can also be served at room temperature.

Autumn in Finland
Pekka Luukkola / VisitFinland.com

HOW TO FOLD

Combining two mixtures by folding is an important technique utilized in baking. It is used with beaten egg whites and with whipped cream to combine without deflating.

When folding, place the lighter mixture on top and use a rubber spatula. Draw the spatula vertically down through the middle and under the mixture, across the bottom of the bowl and pull up on the side. Turn the bowl a quarter turn and repeat until the two mixtures are combined. The down, across, up and over motion keeps the mixture light and airy.

Rhubarb Cake with Lemon Butter Sauce

Tender bright red stalks of rhubarb are available in the spring and early summer. During the rest of the year, you can purchase frozen rhubarb but the stalks are usually thick. Chop frozen stalks so the sharp tangy fruit flavor is evenly distributed. For a rich buttery sauce like this, use freshly squeezed lemon juice.

MAKES 9 SERVINGS

2 cups	all-purpose flour		1 cup	2% milk
1 cup + 1 tablespoon	sugar		3 tablespoons	butter, melted
2 teaspoons	baking powder		1 cup	chopped rhubarb
1/4 teaspoon	salt		1 teaspoon	cinnamon

SAUCE

1 cup	sugar		3/4 cup	heavy whipping cream
1/2 cup	butter		2 tablespoons (1 lemon)	lemon juice

Heat the oven to 375° F. Lightly grease a 9" x 9" baking dish or spray with nonstick cooking spray.

Combine flour, 1 cup sugar, baking powder and salt in a medium bowl. Add milk and butter and whisk until smooth. Stir in the rhubarb. Pour into the prepared pan.

Combine the remaining 1 tablespoon sugar and the cinnamon in a small dish. Sprinkle over the batter.

Bake 30 to 40 minutes or until wooden pick inserted in the center comes out clean. Cool slightly on a wire cooling rack.

Make the sauce. Combine the sugar, butter and whipping cream in a small saucepan. Bring to a boil over medium high heat, stirring constantly. Reduce the heat to low and simmer 5 minutes or until slightly thickened, stirring occasionally. Stir in the lemon juice. Serve the sauce warm or refrigerate until needed.

Borgund Stave Church
Johan Berge / Innovation Norway

STAVE CHURCHES

Stave churches, originally built in the 11th century, are Norway's most significant architectural contribution to design.

Staves were cut from pine trees that were specially grown for strength and durability. After construction, the wood was coated with tar for preservation. Stave churches are tall and skinny with Viking-style gargoyles and carvings. The doors and frames were elaborately carved with dragons entwined with stems and vines and are considered some of the most distinctive art in Norway.

Those churches built in the 11th century fell victim to wood rot because the staves were set directly into the ground. In the 12th century, the staves were set into a stone foundation. Today 28 of the approximately 1000 surviving stave churches have been restored and are considered part of the national heritage.

Strawberry Cream Cake

Bakers in all of the Scandinavian countries create an airy sponge cake like this to showcase the first strawberries of the season. Custard filling is sometimes spread between the layers. Save a few perfect berries for a garnish.

MAKES **10** TO **12** SERVINGS

3/4 cup	cake flour	1/4 teaspoon	salt	
3/4 cup + 1 tablespoon	sugar	1/4 teaspoon	cream of tartar	
4	large eggs, room temperature	1 tablespoon	water	
		1 teaspoon	vanilla	

TOPPING

3 cups	chopped strawberries, 1/2" pieces	1 1/2 cups	confectioners' sugar, sifted	
1 tablespoon	sugar	1 teaspoon	vanilla	
1/2 pkg (4 ounces)	cream cheese, softened	1 1/2 cups	heavy whipping cream	

Heat the oven to 350° F. Line the bottom of two 9" round cake pans with parchment paper or waxed paper. Spray the paper lightly with nonstick cooking spray. Sift the cake flour with 1 tablespoon sugar.

Place the eggs, 3/4 cup sugar, salt, cream of tartar, water and vanilla in a large mixer bowl. Beat on high with a whisk attachment until thick and lemon colored, about 5 minutes. When the whisk is lifted, the eggs will form a thick ribbon that dissolves.

Fold in the cake flour (see *How to Fold*, page 39) and mix until blended. Pour into the prepared pans and spread evenly. Bake 13 to 16 minutes or until the center springs back when touched lightly with a finger.

Cool pans 10 minutes on a wire cooling rack. Run a thin metal spatula around the edges of the pans loosening the cake. Carefully remove the cakes from pans and peel off the parchment paper. Cool completely on the wire cooling rack.

Make the topping. Mix the strawberries with the sugar in a medium bowl and let stand 5 minutes. Beat the cream cheese, confectioners' sugar and vanilla in a large mixer bowl on high with a whisk attachment until creamy. Scrape down the sides of the bowl. Gradually add the whipping cream while beating on low. Increase speed to high and continue beating until soft peaks form. Beat in strawberries and beat about 30 seconds.

Place one layer of the cake on a serving dish. Spread with 2 cups strawberry whipped cream, spreading to the edges. Add the second layer and cover with the remaining strawberry whipped cream. Chill at least 2 hours before serving. Garnish with additional strawberries, if desired. Cake must be refrigerated.

Midsummer Procession
Yanan Li / Stockholm Visitors Board

MIDSUMMER

Midsummer is celebrated in all of the Scandinavian countries and is equal in popularity to Christmas.

Most Midsummer Eve festivities take place on the Saturday between June 20th and June 26th to coordinate with the summer solstice, the beginning of the brief summer season. Swedish "Midsommar" begins the evening before because Swedes enjoy celebrating holidays on Fridays.

Scandinavians decorate their houses with flower garlands and wreaths and in the evening, dances are held around a maypole.

In Denmark and Norway, Midsummer is marked with bonfires and processions. Each region of Sweden has its traditional costume and Midsommar is the occasion when they are most likely to be worn.

For a proper feast, pickled herring and potatoes with fresh dill are essential and are often followed by the first strawberries of the season topped with whipped cream.

Mini Princess Cakes

Princess Cake is a Swedish favorite and present at many special occasions such as birthdays, baptisms and graduations. There are several steps to this recipe but the end results will reward your efforts. I like making individual cakes because they are easier to cover with the pale green marzipan which is surprisingly easy to roll out.

MAKES 6 CAKES

1/2 cup	cake flour		1/4 teaspoon	cream of tartar
1/2 cup	sugar, divided		1 tablespoon	water
1/4 teaspoon	salt		1 teaspoon	vanilla
2	large eggs, room temperature			

FILLING

1/3 cup	sugar		1	large egg, well beaten
2 tablespoons	cornstarch		1 tablespoon	butter
1/8 teaspoon	salt		1 teaspoon	vanilla
1 cup	whole milk			
1 cup	heavy whipping cream		2 (8 ounce) cans	marzipan
2 tablespoons	sugar		Green or pink food coloring	
1 1/2 cups	fresh raspberries			

Heat the oven to 350° F. Spray the cups in a jumbo 6-cup muffin pan with nonstick cooking spray with flour. Sift the cake flour with 1 tablespoon sugar.

Place 2 eggs, the remaining sugar, salt, cream of tartar, water and vanilla in a large mixer bowl. Beat on high with a whisk attachment until thick and lemon colored, about 5 minutes. When the whisk is lifted, the eggs will form a thick ribbon that dissolves. Fold in the cake flour (see *How to Fold*, page 39) and mix just until blended. Pour into the 6 muffin cups and spread evenly. Bake 22 to 26 minutes or until the center springs back when touched lightly with a finger.

Cool the pans 10 minutes on a wire cooling rack. Run a thin metal spatula around the edges of the cakes to loosen. Carefully invert the cakes onto a wire cooling rack. Cool completely.

Make the filling. Combine the sugar, cornstarch and salt in a heavy saucepan. Slowly stir in the milk and continue stirring until the cornstarch dissolves. Cook over medium heat, stirring constantly, until sauce thickens and comes to a boil. Reduce the heat to low and continue to cook 1 minute, stirring constantly.

Remove the pan from the heat. Place the beaten egg in a medium bowl and slowly pour 1/2 cup hot filling into the bowl, beating constantly until smooth. Gradually pour the warmed mixture back into the hot filling while whisking or stirring rapidly. Return pan to heat and cook on low, stirring constantly, about 1 minute or until mixture thickens. Do not let filling boil or eggs will curdle.

Stir in butter and vanilla. Remove from heat and cool. To keep a skin from forming, press a piece of plastic wrap on the surface of the filling. When cool, store in the refrigerator 4 hours or overnight before using.

Girls Gathering Flowers
Marte Kopperud / Innovation Norway

SWEDISH PRINCESS CAKE

The origin of the Swedish Princess Cake isn't clear but many think it was named for the three daughters of Prince Karl and Princess Ingeborg of Sweden.

The recipe, first published in a 1930's cookbook, is thought to be a combination of three cakes, each a favorite of one princess. The delicate sponge cake is usually covered with a layer of marzipan, tinted a pale green, and often topped with a pink rose garnish.

Beat whipping cream in large mixer bowl with whisk attachment until stiff peaks form. Reduce mixer to low and beat in sugar.

Cut cakes horizontally in half. Spread 3 tablespoons filling on the cut surface of the bottom half. Cover with raspberries. Spread 1 to 2 tablespoons whipped cream over raspberries. Cover with the top of the cake. Spread sides with whipped cream, mounding on top. Place in refrigerator while preparing marzipan.

Add 2 to 3 drops green food color to each can of marzipan and knead until evenly mixed. Divide each can into 3 pieces. Lightly dust a work surface and rolling pin with confectioners' sugar. Roll each piece to a 6" circle. Gently shape over each cake, trimming the edges. Store in the refrigerator.

Norwegian Toscakake

To Scandinavians "tosca" means a layer of sliced almonds covered with a buttery caramel topping. The tender sponge cake is leavened mostly by air beaten into the eggs and is typical of the type of cakes popular in Scandinavia. Toasting the almonds brings out their nutty flavor and adds color to the topping.

MAKES 8 SERVINGS

1 1/4 cups	all-purpose flour		1/2 cup	sugar
1/2 teaspoon	baking powder		1/2 cup	butter, melted and cooled
1/4 teaspoon	salt		1 teaspoon	almond extract
4	large eggs, separated, room temperature			

TOPPING

1/2 cup	sugar		3/4 cup	sliced almonds, toasted
2 tablespoons	all-purpose flour		1/2 teaspoon	almond extract
1/2 cup	butter			
2 tablespoons	2% milk			

Heat the oven to 350° F. Lightly grease or spray with nonstick cooking spray the bottom and sides of a 9" springform pan.

Combine the flour, baking powder and salt in a medium bowl.

Beat the whites in a mixer bowl with the whisk attachment until foamy. Gradually beat in the sugar and continue beating until stiff peaks form, about 5 minutes. Place in another bowl.

Whip the egg yolks in the mixer bowl with the whisk attachment until they are light and lemon colored, about 4 minutes. Fold the egg whites (see *How to Fold*, page 39) into the egg yolks using a light touch.

Gently fold in the flour mixture in 4 batches. Fold in the butter and almond extract. Pour into the prepared springform pan.

Bake 22 to 25 minutes or until cake springs back when lightly touched in the center and begins to pull away from the sides of the pan. Remove from the oven. Heat broiler to high.

While the cake is baking, combine the sugar and flour for the topping in a small saucepan. Add the butter and milk and cook over low heat, stirring constantly, until thickened, 1 to 2 minutes. Stir in the almonds and almond extract.

Pour the topping over the cake and place under the broiler. Broil until the topping is golden brown, about 1 to 2 minutes.

Cool on a wire cooling rack 5 minutes. Run a metal spatula around the side of the pan to loosen. Remove the side of the pan. Cool completely.

Sunset Over Fjord and Mountains
Kenneth Reynolds

HOW TO BEAT EGG WHITES

It is essential when beating egg whites that there is no yolk present. Separate the eggs when they are cold and allow them to come to room temperature before beating.

Beating the egg whites first and then stabilizing the mixture with sugar allows you to transfer it to another bowl and reuse the mixer bowl and whisk without washing.

Stiff peaks stand up when the beater is lifted. With a circular motion, gently fold the egg whites into the yolk mixture which helps maintain the greatest volume.

Hazelnut Cake with Chocolate Ganache

Ganache is a combination of chocolate and heavy whipping cream. Use high quality chocolate and chop it finely. I always use solid chocolate when I'm making a ganache or glaze because chocolate chips contain stabilizers and don't melt smoothly.

Nyhavn Waterfront in Copenhagen
Nicolai Perjesi / Danish Media Center

MAKES 10 TO 12 SERVINGS

3/4 cup	all-purpose flour		1/2 cup	2% milk
1/4 teaspoon	baking powder		1/2 cup	ground toasted hazelnuts (filberts)
2	large eggs, room temperature		2 tablespoons	butter, melted
3/4 cup	sugar		1/2 teaspoon	vanilla

CHOCOLATE GANACHE

4 ounces	semisweet chocolate, chopped		2 tablespoons	butter
			1 teaspoon	light corn syrup
3 tablespoons	heavy whipping cream		1/2 teaspoon	vanilla

Heat the oven to 350° F. Grease and flour a 9" x 5" loaf pan or line the bottom with parchment paper or waxed paper. Sift the flour and baking powder together.

Place the eggs in a large mixer bowl and gradually beat in the sugar using low speed and a whisk attachment. Increase the speed to high and beat until thick and lemon colored, about 5 minutes. When the whisk is lifted, the eggs will form a thick ribbon that folds back on itself.

Reduce mixer speed to low. Add the flour mixture in 3 additions, alternating with 2 additions of milk, scraping down the sides of the bowl after each addition. After adding all of the flour beat until smooth, but no longer than 15 seconds. Fold in the hazelnuts, butter and vanilla (see *How to Fold*, page 39).

Pour into the prepared pan and spread evenly. Bake 35 to 40 minutes or until the center springs back when touched lightly with a finger.

Cool the cake 10 minutes on a wire cooling rack. Run a thin metal spatula around the sides of the pan, loosening the cake. Carefully remove the cake from the pan. Cool completely on the wire cooling rack.

Make the ganache. Combine the chocolate, whipping cream and butter in a small saucepan. Heat over low heat about 2 minutes, stirring occasionally, until smooth. Stir in the corn syrup and vanilla. Let cool until thick enough to spread, about 30 minutes.

Spread the ganache over the top of the cake allowing it to drip down the sides. Allow to stand a couple of hours for the ganache to set. Don't refrigerate or the ganache will lose it shine.

HAZELNUTS

Hazelnuts, also called filberts, grow on a bush found throughout Europe and usually ripen around August 22nd, the Feast of St. Philbert.

Hazelnuts are covered with a thin brown skin that is very bitter and should be removed before using. Sometimes you can buy hazelnuts that already have the skin removed.

To remove the skin, place the nuts on a baking sheet and bake in a 350° F oven 10 to 15 minutes or until the skins begin to crack. Wrap the warm nuts in a clean dishtowel and let cool 5 minutes. Rub the nuts together vigorously in the towel to remove the skins.

Hazelnuts are high in heart-healthy monoun-saturated fats, vitamin E and minerals and make a healthy addition to foods, especially cakes and cookies.

Orange Bundt Cake

A classic pound cake is made with one pound each of butter, sugar, eggs and flour but doesn't have the lighter texture preferred today in cakes. The delicate orange flavor added by the orange rind can be intensified by also adding orange extract. If you are using a fluted tube pan, I recommend using shortening and brushing it into all the grooves in the pan before flouring.

MAKES 1 CAKE, 12 TO 16 SERVINGS

2 1/2 cups	all-purpose flour	4	large eggs, room temperature
1/2 teaspoon	baking powder		
1/2 teaspoon	baking soda	1 teaspoon	vanilla
1/2 teaspoon	salt	1 teaspoon	orange extract, if desired
1 cup	unsalted butter, softened	3/4 cup	2% milk, room temperature
1 cup	granulated sugar		
1 cup	firmly packed light brown sugar	1/4 cup	orange juice
		2 tablespoons	grated orange rind

Heat the oven to 350° F with rack in lower third. Thoroughly grease and flour a 10-inch fluted tube pan or an angel food cake pan.

Sift the flour, baking powder, baking soda and salt into a medium bowl. Combine the milk and orange juice.

Beat the butter in the bowl of a heavy-duty mixer on medium speed until creamy. Gradually add the granulated sugar and brown sugar, scraping down the sides of the bowl occasionally, and beat 2 minutes.

Beat in the eggs, one at a time, scraping the sides of the bowl after each egg is added. Add the vanilla and orange extract and beat 3 minutes until the mixture is very light and creamy.

Reduce the mixer speed to low. Add the flour mixture in 3 additions, alternating with 2 additions of the milk. Scrape down the sides of the bowl after each addition. After adding all of the flour beat until smooth, but no longer than 15 seconds.

Stir in the orange juice and orange rind. Pour into the prepared pan and spread evenly.

Bake 50 to 60 minutes or until a toothpick inserted in the center of cake comes out clean. Cool on a wire cooling rack 10 minutes. Run a spatula or a wooden skewer around the edge of the pan and around tube in the center to loosen the cake. Carefully loosen the cake from pan and invert onto cooling rack. Cool completely.

Serve with whipped cream.

Dining Room at Amalienborg Palace
Dorte Krogh / Denmark Media Center

AMALIENBORG PALACE

Amalienborg Palace, the residence of Danish monarchs, is named after Queen Sophie Amalie who had a small palace on the site in 1689. The area is also known as Frederickstaten for King Frederick V who directed the development of the Square.

The site for the four palaces was given to four prominent noblemen, who committed themselves to building identical palaces, designed by the court architect Nicolai Eigtved. Today one of the palaces on the grounds, Schacks Manor, is the home of Queen Margrethe II during the winter. The changing of the guards occurs every day when the Queen is in residence.

Glazed Lemon Pound Cake

Grated lemon rind gives the delicate lemon flavor to this dessert and freshly squeezed lemon juice adds tanginess. Be sure you remove the rind before cutting the lemon in half to squeeze out the juice. I've found that a microplane grater makes removing rind easy and is a utensil I use often.

MAKES 1 CAKE, 10 TO 12 SERVINGS EACH

1 1/2 cups	all-purpose flour		1/2 teaspoon	vanilla
1/2 teaspoon	baking powder		1/2 cup	whole milk, room temperature
1/4 teaspoon	salt		1 tablespoon	grated lemon rind
1/2 cup	unsalted butter, softened		1 cup	confectioners' sugar, sifted
1	cup sugar		2 tablespoons (1 lemon)	lemon juice
2	large eggs, room temperature			

Heat the oven to 350° F with rack in lower third. Grease and flour a 9" x 5" loaf pan.

Sift the flour, baking powder and salt into a medium bowl.

Beat the butter in the bowl of a heavy-duty mixer on medium speed until creamy. Gradually add the sugar, scraping down the sides of the bowl occasionally, and beat 2 minutes.

Beat in the eggs, one at a time, scraping the sides of the bowl after each egg is added. Add the vanilla and beat 3 minutes until the mixture is very light and creamy.

Reduce the mixer speed to low. Add the flour mixture in 3 additions, alternating with 2 additions of the milk. Scrape down the sides of the bowl after each addition. After adding all of the flour beat until smooth, but no longer than 15 seconds.

Stir in the lemon rind. Pour into the prepared pan and spread evenly.

Bake 45 to 55 minutes or until a toothpick inserted in the center of cake comes out clean. Cool on a wire cooling rack 10 minutes. Invert onto the rack.

Beat the confectioners' sugar and lemon juice for the glaze until smooth. Pour over the warm cake. Cool completely.

Finnish Ice Bar
VF Kemi / VisitFinland.com

AQUAVIT

The word "aquavit" comes from the Latin "aqua vitae" meaning "water of life." It is popular in Sweden, Norway and Denmark. Finland prefers vodka, probably because it shares a border with Russia.

Aquavit is distilled from grain or potatoes and flavored with caraway, dill, cumin or other herbs or spices. It is usually 42% to 45% alcohol by volume. In the Scandinavian countries it is thought to aid in the digestion of heavy or rich foods and is important to many holidays such as Christmas in Denmark, Midsommar in Sweden and Constitution Day in Norway. It is meant to go with food such as shrimp and herring, especially at a Swedish smorgasbord or Danish cold table. "Drinking snaps" is a cultural tradition and a formal procedure.

Aquavit is usually served very cold in a stemmed glass except in Norway where it is served at room temperature. A Norwegian specialty "linje akavits" is carried across the equator two times in an oak barrel in the hold of a ship. Some say this changes it by extracting more flavor from the casks but others think that's just a marketing tool.

SCANDINAVIAN COOKIES

UNEXPECTED GUESTS are always welcomed with coffee and cookies in Scandinavian homes. That's the reason most of their cookie recipes make many dozens of cookies. A variety of rich buttery cookies are always ready for unplanned company.

Most cookies are baked on ungreased baking sheets because the butter in the dough prevents them from sticking. Only grease baking sheets when it's specified in the recipe or the cookies may spread too much. Use parchment paper to line the baking sheet for easy clean-up, using the paper several times.

Some of the cookies in this chapter are shaped into balls. I've found the easiest way to measure the dough accurately is to use a cookie scoop. Drop the dough onto the baking sheet and then roll into balls.

The mother of a friend of mine was famous for the beautiful and elegant trays of Swedish cookies she served, especially during the holidays. The Desert Sand Cookies recipe is from her recipe box. Browned butter has a delectable nutty, not burnt, flavor. Browning the butter gives the cookies a sandy-mouth feel, hence their name. The Finnish Teaspoon Cookies also contain browned butter and are unique because they are shaped into ovals using the bowl of a teaspoon.

Holiday Cottage on the Lake
Krista Keltanen / VisitFinland.com

Scandinavian Apricot Almond Bars

A pastry blender makes it easy to combine flour and butter for the crust and results in flaky layers. You can also use two knives and a scissor-like motion to get the same result. Don't leave large pieces of butter or holes will form when they melt.

MAKES 24 TO 30 BARS

CRUST

2 cups	all-purpose flour		3/4 cup	butter
1 cup	confectioners' sugar			

TOPPING

3/4 cup	apricot preserves		1 teaspoon	almond extract
2	egg whites		1/2 cup	slivered almonds, toasted
1 cup	confectioners' sugar			

Heat the oven to 350° F. Line the bottom of a 13" x 9" baking pan with aluminum foil, extending the foil over the long sides of the pan. Lightly spray the foil with nonstick cooking spray.

Combine the flour, confectioners' sugar and butter for the crust in a large bowl. Cut in the butter with a pastry blender until mixture resembles coarse crumbs. Press into the baking pan, pressing about 1/2" up the sides.

Bake 15 to 20 minutes or until the edges begin to brown.

While the crust is baking, toast the almonds. Place the almonds on a small baking dish and bake about 8 minutes.

Beat the egg whites with a whisk until foamy. Beat in the confectioners' sugar and almond extract.

Spread the apricot preserves over the crust. Spoon the egg whites over the preserves without covering the preserves completely. Sprinkle with the almonds.

Bake 15 to 18 minutes or until the topping is golden brown. Run a metal spatula along the short sides of the pan to loosen the pastry. Cool completely on a wire cooling rack. Using the foil, lift the pastry from the pan and cut into 24 bars.

To cut diamonds, cut lengthwise into 6 strips. Make parallel diagonal cuts on each strip to form diamonds.

Oresund Bridge at Sunset
Henrik Stenberg / Danish Media Center

ORESUND BRIDGE

The Oresund Bridge, a ten-mile span with four lanes for traffic and two railroad tracks, opened to public traffic in 2000. The bridge connects Copenhagen, Denmark and Malmo, Sweden.

Creating a link between Western and Central Europe and Scandinavia, over 25 million people have crossed it since its opening. The Oresund Bridge has the longest underwater tube tunnel and the longest cable-supported bridge span in the world. The construction of the bridge was complicated by the decision to create an underwater tunnel on one end in order to prevent interference with air traffic approaching the Copenhagen airport and to keep a clear channel open for ships

Today, many commute over the bridge daily to the metropolitan area of Copenhagen taking advantage of lower housing costs in Sweden.

Scandinavian Tosca Squares

MAKES **36** SQUARES

CRUST

1 1/4 cups	all-purpose flour	1/2 cup	butter,
3/4 cup	confectioners' sugar		cut into 1/2" pieces

TOPPING

1/2 cup	sugar	1/4 teaspoon	almond extract
1 tablespoon	all-purpose flour	1/2 cup	sliced almonds,
3 tablespoons	butter		toasted
3 tablespoons	heavy whipping cream or whole milk	2 ounces	semisweet chocolate, finely chopped

Heat the oven to 400° F. Combine the flour and confectioners' sugar for the crust in a medium bowl. Cut in the butter with a pastry blender until mixture resembles coarse crumbs. Press the dough into a 9" x 9" baking pan. Bake 12 to 15 minutes or until the edges begin to brown.

Mix the sugar and 1 tablespoon flour in a small saucepan. Add the butter and whipping cream. Bring the mixture to a boil. Reduce the heat to medium and cook 2 minutes stirring constantly. Remove the pan from the heat and stir in the almonds and almond extract. Pour over the warm crust.

Bake 10 to 14 minutes or until the topping is bubbling. Place the pan on a wire rack. Run a spatula around the edge to release the pastry. Cool slightly.

Melt the semisweet chocolate in a small pan over low heat or in the microwave. Drizzle over the pastry. Cool completely and cut into squares.

Chocolate Butter Logs

MAKES **3** DOZEN LOGS

2 cups	all-purpose flour	4 ounces	semisweet or white chocolate, chopped
1/3 cup	unsweetened cocoa		
3/4 cup	unsalted butter, softened	1 cup	chopped hazelnuts (see page 49) or almonds, toasted
1 1/2 cups	confectioners' sugar		
1	large egg		
1 1/2 teaspoons	vanilla		

Heat the oven to 375° F. Combine the flour and cocoa in a small bowl and stir until well mixed.

Beat the butter and sugar in a large mixer bowl with electric mixer on medium speed until creamy. Beat in the egg and vanilla.

With the mixer on low speed, add the flour mixture and beat until a soft dough is formed.

Place the dough on a lightly floured surface and divide into thirds. Shape each third into a log about 1/2" across and 18" long. Cut into 3" lengths. Place on baking sheets. If the dough is too soft to handle, chill about 1/2 hour.

Bake 7 to 8 minutes or until set. Cool on wire cooling racks.

Melt the semisweet chocolate in a small pan over low heat or in the microwave. Dip the ends in melted chocolate and roll in chopped hazelnuts or almonds. You can also simply sprinkle the logs with confectioners' sugar.

Danish Almond Cookies

MAKES 3 DOZEN COOKIES

1 1/2 cups	all-purpose flour	1/2 cup	sugar
1/4 teaspoon	baking soda	1	large egg yolk
1/4 teaspoon	cream of tartar	1/2 teaspoon	vanilla
1/2 cup	butter, softened	1/2 teaspoon	almond extract
1/4 cup	vegetable shortening	36	whole almonds

Heat the oven to 350° F. Combine the flour, baking soda and cream of tartar and stir until well mixed.

Beat the butter and shortening in a large mixer bowl with electric mixer on medium speed until creamy. Beat in the sugar and egg yolk and mix well.

With the mixer on low speed, add the flour mixture. Beat until a soft dough is formed.

Shape rounded teaspoons of dough into balls and place on a baking sheet. If the dough is too soft to handle, chill for 30 minutes. Place an almond in the center of each cookie.

Bake 11 to 14 minutes or until edges are lightly browned. Let cookies cool on the baking sheet 1 to 2 minutes. Remove and cool on wire cooling racks.

Desert Sand Cookies

MAKES 3 DOZEN COOKIES

1 cup	butter	1 cup	sugar
2 cups	all-purpose flour	1/2 teaspoon	vanilla
1/2 teaspoon	baking powder		

Brown the butter by melting in a medium saucepan over medium heat. Stir occasionally. When the butter begins to foam, stir constantly until it turns a deep golden brown. Watch carefully because at this point the color changes quickly. It takes about 7 minutes to brown the butter.

Cool to room temperature, about 1 hour.

Heat the oven to 350° F. Mix the flour and baking powder together. Add the cooled butter and vanilla to the sugar in a medium bowl and stir until evenly mixed. Add the flour and mix to form a dough.

Shape the dough into balls using rounded teaspoons of dough. Place on baking sheets and press a crisscross pattern with a fork. Dip the tines of the fork in a little flour if the dough sticks.

Bake 10 to 12 minutes. These cookies do not brown much, so touch them lightly to see if they are set. Cool the cookies on the baking sheet for 2 minutes before removing to a wire cooling rack. The cookies are fragile until they cool.

Hazelnut Thumbprint Cookies

When you press a "thumbprint" into the balls of dough, try to keep a slightly raised edge around the center. This will prevent the preserves from leaking out during baking. Chopped almonds are always in my pantry and can be used instead of hazelnuts.

MAKES 4 DOZEN COOKIES

2 cups	all-purpose flour
1/4 teaspoon	salt
1 cup	butter, softened
1/2 cup	sugar
2	large eggs, separated
1 teaspoon	almond extract
2 tablespoons	water
1 cup	finely chopped hazelnuts (see page 49)
1 cup	cherry, strawberry or raspberry preserves

Heat the oven to 350° F. Line a baking sheet with parchment paper or spray lightly with nonstick cooking spray.

Combine the flour and salt in a medium bowl and stir until well mixed.

Beat the butter in a large mixer bowl with electric mixer on medium speed until creamy. Beat in the sugar and egg yolks and mix well. With the mixer on low speed, add the flour mixture. Beat until a soft dough is formed.

Beat the egg whites and water with a whisk or fork in a small bowl until foamy. Shape rounded teaspoons of dough into balls, flatten slightly and roll bottom half in the egg whites. Roll in chopped nuts and place on a baking sheet. (If the dough is too soft to handle, chill about 1/2 hour.) Press an indentation in the cookie using your thumb or the back of a teaspoon.

Bake the cookies 10 minutes or until the edges are lightly browned. Remove from the oven and reshape indentation with the back of a spoon. Fill with 1/2 teaspoon cherry preserves.

Continue baking 6 to 8 minutes or until the edges are browned. Let cookies cool on the baking sheet 1 to 2 minutes. Remove and cool on wire cooling racks.

Fjord with Flowers
Frithjof Fure / Innovation Norway

FJORDS

The fjords of western Norway are millions of years old and were formed as glaciers moved toward the sea, gouging out valleys with high mountains on both sides. As the Ice Age ended, the glaciers melted and water filled the valleys creating the extraordinary beauty of today. Norway's fjords are on the UNESCO World Heritage List.

The Sognefjord is 120 miles long and one mile deep, making it one of the largest fjords. Three thousand foot mountains crested with snow surround it, and small and large waterfalls appear along its length. As you sail through the Sognefjord you will see seals and porpoises frolicking in the clear green waters and eagles soaring above. Another famous fjord is the Geirangerfjord, known for the beauty of its waterfalls. The warm Gulf Stream keeps the climate temperate and ice-free.

Because of the fertile soil, the land has been farmed for thousands of years, and the countryside is dotted with farms.

Swedish Almond Rusk

Cardamom is a flavor that is unfamiliar to many but is used often in Scandinavian baking. Freshly ground, it adds a distinctive flavor to rusks but cinnamon can be used as a substitute.

MAKES 3 DOZEN RUSKS

3 1/2 cups	all-purpose flour	1/2 cup	butter, softened
1 teaspoon	baking powder	1 cup	sugar
1 teaspoon	ground cardamom, if desired	1/2 cup	sour cream
1/2 teaspoon	baking soda	1 teaspoon	almond extract
1/4 teaspoon	salt	2	large eggs, beaten
		1/2 cup	chopped almonds

Heat the oven to 350° F. Line a baking sheet with parchment paper or grease thoroughly. Combine the flour, baking powder, cardamom, baking soda and salt in a medium bowl.

Beat the butter in a large mixer bowl with electric mixer on medium speed until creamy. Gradually add sugar and beat 1 minute until light. Beat in the sour cream, almond extract and eggs. With the mixer on low speed, gradually add the flour and beat until a soft dough forms. Beat in the almonds.

Divide the dough into 3 parts. Shape each third into a log about 12" long and 1 1/2" to 2" wide. Place the logs on the baking sheet. Flatten slightly.

Bake 25 to 30 minutes or until lightly browned and firm to the touch. Remove from the oven and cool slightly on the baking sheet.

Cut each log into diagonal slices about 3/4" thick using a serrated knife or a bread knife. Place the slices flat on a baking sheet and return to the oven. Bake 8 to 10 minutes or until toasted. Turn the slices over and continue baking 8 to 10 minutes or until the second side is toasted. Cool on a wire cooling rack.

Café on the Plaza
Olof Holdar / Stockholm Visitors Board

FIKA

"Let's go out for coffee" or "fika" is heard often in Sweden, as the Swedish are possibly the most enthusiastic coffee drinkers in the world. Some think it is the inspiration for the American "coffee break." It may have begun in Wisconsin when wives of immigrants agreed to work in a factory as long as they were allowed to take breaks to talk to their friends and, of course, drink coffee.

In Sweden, coffee and cinnamon rolls are essential for fika as are cookies or sweet rolls. Some hostesses feel that at least three baked items are needed when inviting friends for fika.

Fika is usually in the morning or afternoon and is a way for families and friends to catch up. It can also mean going on a date, although the custom is less popular with young people.

Finnish Browned Butter Teaspoon Cookies

Buttery and tangy, these cookies are always popular on buffets or cookie trays during the holidays. Experiment on the easiest way to press out the cookies using the bowl of a teaspoon and forming the delicate oval shape. The dough is easy to shape because it's slightly dry.

Makes 24 sandwich cookies

1 cup	butter		1 tablespoon	vanilla
2 cups	all-purpose flour		1/3 cup	raspberry or
1/2 teaspoon	baking soda			strawberry jam
3/4 cup	sugar		Confectioners' sugar	

Brown the butter by melting in a medium saucepan over medium heat. Stir occasionally. When butter begins to foam up, stir constantly until it turns a deep golden brown. Watch carefully because at this point, the color changes quickly. It takes about 7 minutes to brown the butter. Cool to room temperature, about 1 hour.

Heat the oven to 325° F.

Mix the flour and baking soda together.

Combine the cooled butter, sugar and vanilla in a medium bowl and stir until evenly mixed. Add the flour and mix to form a dough.

Shape the cookies by placing about 1 teaspoon of dough into the bowl of a teaspoon and pressing against the side of the bowl, leveling the top. Press out cookie, flat side down, onto an ungreased baking sheet.

Bake 10 to 13 minutes or until lightly browned and set. Let cool on the baking sheet for 2 minutes and remove to a wire cooling rack.

When cookies are cool, spread a scant 1/2 teaspoon of jam on the flat side of one cookie. Make a sandwich by pressing the flat side of a second cookie onto the jam. Sprinkle the sandwiches with confectioners' sugar.

Sauna on the Water
Christer Lundin / Stockholm Visitors Board

Saunas

Saunas, an important part of Finnish culture, have been in use at least a thousand years and are still popular today as a place to relax with friends and family. Finland, a country with a population of around five million, has over a million saunas.

Originally saunas were a place to bathe but because they are very clean, they were also used for giving birth and as a place for healing the sick.

A traditional sauna is a wood-paneled room with a wood-fired stove covered with rocks. Adding water to the hot rocks produces steam, cleansing the body through sweat. Birch branches can add to the effect of a sauna when they are used to gently beat oneself, relaxing muscles and opening sinuses with the aroma of chlorophyll.

When you become very hot from the sauna, you can then stand under an icy shower, roll in the snow or jump into a crystal clear lake. Then, you can do it all again!

SCANDINAVIAN TARTS,
FRUIT DESSERTS
& PASTRIES

FRUIT DESSERTS capture the bright flavors of summer berries or the crispness of autumn apples. Many Scandinavian classic desserts depend on fresh seasonal produce. One of the best ways to savor seasonal berries is by baking them into tarts or crumbles. Rhubarb, a sure sign of spring, is popular for its sharp tangy flavor, especially when balanced by rich whipped cream.

The pastry that lines the tart pans for the Blueberry Tart and Rhubarb Tarts is one of my favorites because it doesn't have to be rolled but is easily pressed into the pans. Once you buy 3" tart pans (see *Sources*, page 96), you'll be surprised as how often you use them.

The Meringue with Peaches and Raspberries and the Danish Pastries take time to make but the directions are clearly written. For details on how to beat egg whites for meringue, see *How to Beat Egg Whites*, page 47. Danish Pastry needs to chill several times during the folding process but this is what makes the flaky layers and is worth the extra time. Handle the dough gently and you'll be proud of your results. I've chosen the simplest way of shaping the filled pastries but you can shape the dough many different ways.

Village Reflected in the Fjord
Jens Henrik Nybo / Innovation Norway

Blueberry Tart

Every summer when fresh local blueberries arrive in the farmers' market, I make this simple tart. It's important to grease the tart pan so the sweet crust doesn't stick. Rather than rolling out the crust, just press it into the pan. I try to heap some berries in the center because they collapse when they are baked, but don't overdo it or the filling will overflow.

MAKE 8 SERVINGS

CRUST

1 1/4 cups	all-purpose flour		1/2 cup	unsalted cold butter, cut into 1/2" pieces
1/4 cup	sugar		1	large egg yolk
1/4 teaspoon	salt			

FILLING

3 1/2 cups	fresh blueberries		2 tablespoons	all-purpose flour
3/4 cup	sugar		1 teaspoon	cinnamon

CRUMB TOPPING

1/3 cup	sugar		3 tablespoons	unsalted butter
1/3 cup	all-purpose flour			

Heat the oven to 400° F. Using shortening, grease the bottom and sides of a 9" tart pan with a removeable bottom and dust well with flour. (You may place the pan on a parchment paper-lined baking sheet to catch drips.)

Make the crust. Combine the flour, sugar and salt for the crust in a food processor bowl. Add the cold butter and pulse until mixture resembles coarse crumbs with some pea-sized pieces. Scrape down the sides of the bowl. With the processor running, add the egg yolk. Process until dough starts to clump together. This will take about 15 seconds. If large clumps do not form, add water a teaspoon at a time.

Put the dough on a lightly floured surface and gather into a ball. Place the dough in center of the prepared tart pan. Using your fingers, press dough out to the edges of the pan and all the way up the sides. Lightly dust your fingers with a little flour if dough is sticky.

Make the filling. Combine blueberries, sugar, flour and cinnamon in a large bowl. Spoon into the tart pan mounding the blueberries in the center. The pan will be very full but the berries shrink with baking.

Make the crumb topping. Combine the sugar and flour for the topping in a small bowl. Cut in the butter with a pastry blender until coarse crumbs form. Sprinkle over the blueberries.

Bake 50 to 60 minutes or until filling is bubbling all over and sugar has dissolved. Cool on wire cooling rack at least 2 hours before cutting.

Serve with whipped cream or ice cream.

Gamla Stan in the Evening
Preben Kristensen / Stockholm Visitors Board

GAMLA STAN

Gamla stan (the Old Town) is located in Stockholm on the island of Stadsholmen. Because it includes the islands of Riddarholmen and Helgeandsholmen, it has also been called the "town between the bridges." It is where the city of Stockholm was founded in 1252 and is one of the best preserved medieval centers in Europe. Narrow winding alleys, cobbled streets and golden buildings give it a character that is unique.

The population today is about 3,000 people. In the 1980s the area was restored, making it a popular tourist site. Sweden's national cathedral, Stockholm Cathedral, the Royal Palace, which was built in the 18th century, and the Nobel Museum are located here. The Stortorget, the oldest square in Stockholm, marks the beginning of the oldest street in Stockholm, Kopmangatan, dating from the 14th century. Den glydene freden, located here, is the oldest restaurant in the world and has been serving food since 1722.

Rhubarb Tarts

The brilliant red stalks and tart tangy flavor of rhubarb signals that it's spring! For this recipe you need 8 3"-tart pans. I like one-piece tart pans because it can be hard to remove the tarts from the bottom of two-piece tart pans. I use a wooden skewer to loosen the curvy edges of the tart, especially if the filling has run over, making it easier to remove the tarts.

MAKES 8 TARTS

CRUST

1 1/2 cups	all-purpose flour		1/2 cup	cold butter, cut-up
1/2 teaspoon	salt		3 to 4 tablespoons	ice water

FILLING

2 slices	soft white bread, crust removed, cubed		3 tablespoons	all-purpose flour
1/4 cup	butter, melted		2	large eggs, well beaten
1 1/2 cups	sugar		3 1/2 cups	diced rhubarb

Heat the oven to 350° F. Make the crust. Place the flour and salt in a food processor bowl and pulse briefly to mix. Add the butter and process until mixture resembles coarse crumbs with some pea-sized pieces. Scrape down the sides of the bowl. Add 3 tablespoons ice water and process until dough begins to clump together. This will take 10 seconds or longer. If large clumps do not form, add a little more water, 1 teaspoon at a time.

Put the dough on a well-floured work surface, and gather it together into a ball. Divide into 8 pieces. Press each piece into a 3" tart pan, pressing slightly above the top edge of the pan. Place the tarts on a jellyroll pan or cookie sheet lined with parchment paper in case filling runs over the sides.

Make the filling. Toss the bread cubes with the butter until the bread is well coated. Divide into the tart pans.

Combine the sugar and flour in a medium bowl. Stir in the eggs and mix well. Stir in the rhubarb. Divide into the tart pans, evenly distributing the rhubarb.

Bake 30 to 35 minutes or until knife inserted in the center comes out clean. Crusts should be golden brown. Cool tarts on a wire cooling rack. Remove from pans. Serve slightly warm or at room temperature with vanilla ice cream.

Reindeer in Lapland Finland
VisitFinland.com

SMORGASBORD

All Scandinavia countries enjoy an extensive buffet that we call a "smorgasbord." In Denmark it is called "Kolde bord," Norway "koldtbord" and Sweden "smorgasbord." At the 1939 New York World's Fair, a smorgasbord first appeared in the Swedish pavilion's restaurant where it gained international recognition.

A smorgasbord is an elaborate meal, carefully arranged following specific guidelines. It includes at least three courses and each course may have as many as 20 dishes.

In the first course, cold foods are typically displayed on ice accompanied by cheeses and crispbreads. Herring is a star attraction and is served in many different forms. Smoked or cured salmon is also popular. The second course is served at room temperature and includes meats and salads. The third course, which is not always the final course, features hot dishes, such as Swedish meatballs, and cabbage rolls.

Although there are variations from country to country, these impressive buffets are an important part of Scandinavian life.

Swedish Apple Pie

This simple dessert is often called "applekake," apple cake, but it is similar to pie or an apple crisp. The topping is quick to assemble and perfect for a weeknight family dinner. Serve it with a scoop of ice cream and everyone will linger to savor every spoonful.

MAKES 8 SERVINGS

4 cups	sliced, peeled, cored apples (Granny Smith, Gala, Braeburn)		3/4 cup	butter, softened
			1 cup	sugar
			1	large egg, beaten
1/4 cup	firmly packed light brown sugar		1 cup	all-purpose flour
			1/2 cup	chopped walnuts
1 teaspoon	cinnamon			

Heat the oven to 350° F. Butter or lightly spray a 10" deep-dish pie plate.

Combine the apples, brown sugar and cinnamon in a medium bowl and spoon into the prepared dish.

Beat the butter and sugar until smooth. Beat in the egg. Add the flour and beat until smooth. Stir in the walnuts. Spread over the apples.

Bakes 45 to 55 minutes or until the top is golden and the apples are tender. To determine if the apples are tender, pierce a slice of apple with the tip of a knife.

Cut into wedges and serve warm with ice cream or whipped cream.

The Black Diamond, Royal Library
Jogen Schytte / Denmark Media Center

SCANDINAVIAN DESIGN

The underlying principle of Scandinavian design is the idea that beautiful and functional items should be available to all. This clean style first appeared in the 1950s as a part of social democracy and was made possible by readily available low-cost materials and mass production. It is defined by simple designs, minimalism and functionality.

Scandinavian design's main focuses are products for the home. Companies such as IKEA, Marimekko, Iittala, Royal Copenhagen and Electrolux produce products that showcase this ideal. Alvar Aalto's simple laminated stool is a well-known example.

Scandinavia's architects are world famous and include Arne Jacobsen—the godfather of Danish design—who designed the 1960 Radisson SAS Royal Hotel across from Tivoli Gardens, and Dane Jorn Utzon, the designer of the world renowned Sydney Opera House.

Triple Berry Crumble

Capture the fresh flavors of summer's ripe berries by choosing your favorite combination of berries. I like to bake this mouth-watering dessert in a pottery casserole that can go right to the table. Add a scoop of vanilla ice cream or sweetened whipped cream and dig in.

MAKES 8 SERVINGS

FILLING

6 cups	assorted fresh berries (blueberries, raspberries, strawberries, blackberries)	1/2 cup	sugar
		1/4 cup	cornstarch
		3 tablespoons (2 lemons)	lemon juice
		1 tablespoon	grated lemon rind

CRUMBLE

1/2 cup	all-purpose flour	1/4 cup	butter
1/2 cup	firmly packed light brown sugar	1/2 cup	sliced almonds

Heat the oven to 375° F. Make the filling. Place the berries in a large bowl. Combine the sugar and cornstarch in a small bowl and stir into the berries. Stir in the lemon juice and rind. Spoon fruit into a 2-quart baking dish or a 9" x 9" baking pan.

Make the crumble. Combine the flour and brown sugar in a small bowl. Cut into the butter with a pastry blender until mixture resembles coarse crumbs. Stir in the almonds. Sprinkle the crumble over the fruit.

Bake 45 to 55 minutes or until the crumb topping is browned and the juices have thickened. If you are using a deep dish or casserole, you may need to bake a little longer. The juices should be thick and bubbling in the center.

Serve warm or at room temperature.

Viking Play at Jels
Mogens Skou / Denmark Media Center

VIKINGS

The Vikings were great traders, shipbuilders and explorers looking for more prosperous lands. Because of the inhospitality of the land. hunger may have driven some of their voyages. The Vikings learned to smoke, dry and salt their meat and fish in order to undertake these long voyages. In addition to being food for the sailors, dried cod was also a source of trade.

From 400 AD to 1100 AD, the Vikings sailed the Mediterranean, the Baltic and the Black Seas often building settlements in addition to raiding. In about 1000 AD they settled in northern France where they were called Normans or "Northmen."

The Vikings believed that the world was flat and trusted their gods to protect and povide for them. Their vision of heaven included a boar, Saerimne, who was an eternal source of meat.

After sailing into and raiding Roman territory, they became Christians and were assimilated into society leaving their warlike ways behind.

Danish Pastry

In Denmark, these pastries are called "Weinerbrod" or Vienna bread. About 100 years ago when the bakers in Copenhagen went on strike for better wages, Austrian and German bakers were brought to Denmark to replace them. Their Viennese method of folding butter into pastry dough forming many layers was adopted and improved by the Danish bakers when they returned and Danish pastry is now famous throughout the world.

MAKES 24 PASTRIES

DOUGH

3/4 cup	whole milk	1/4 cup	warm water
1/4 cup	sugar		(105° to 115° F.)
3 tablespoons	unsalted butter	1	large egg, beaten
1 1/2 teaspoons	salt	3 to 3 1/2 cups	all-purpose flour
1 (1/4 ounce) pkg	active dry yeast	1 cup	cold unsalted butter

CREAM CHEESE FILLING

1 pkg (8 ounces)	cream cheese, softened	2 to 4 tablespoons	sugar
		1/4 teaspoon	salt
1	large egg, beaten	1 teaspoon	vanilla

ALMOND FILLING

1 can (8 ounces)	almond paste	3 tablespoons sugar
1	large egg white	
1	large egg, beaten	Swedish pearl sugar
1 teaspoon	water	

Bike Race in Denmark
Cees van Roeden / Danish Media Center

Make the dough. Combine the milk, sugar, butter and salt in a medium saucepan and heat over medium heat until small bubbles form on the side of the pan, about 2 to 3 minutes. Remove from the heat and cool to 115° F. The butter doesn't need to melt. Pour into the bowl of a heavy-duty mixer.

Sprinkle the yeast over the warm water and let stand 5 minutes until the yeast is dissolved. Add the yeast and egg to the mixer bowl and stir in 2 cups flour. Beat on medium speed for 3 minutes. Stir in 1 to 1 1/2 cups flour or enough to make a soft dough.

Knead dough 4 to 5 minutes on a lightly floured surface until smooth and elastic. Add flour as needed to prevent dough from sticking. Cover dough and let rest about 45 minutes.

Soften 1 cup butter slightly until it can be spread or roll out it between two pieces of parchment paper. Shape or roll it to a 12" x 16" rectangle and chill 30 minutes.

Roll the dough on a lightly floured surface to a 24" x 12" rectangle, making sure the dough doesn't stick to the surface. Remove the paper from the butter and place short side of butter along the short edge covering 2/3 of the dough. Fold the remaining 1/3 of the dough over the butter and brush off any excess flour. Fold over the final 1/3 of the dough.

Turn the direction of the dough 1/4 turn and roll to a 12" x 24" rectangle. Fold over 1/3 of the dough and cover with the final 1/3. Chill 1 1/2 hours or longer.

Repeat rolling and folding 2 more times. Chill until firm or overnight.

Make the cream cheese filling. Beat the cream cheese until creamy in a medium bowl. Add the egg, sugar, salt and vanilla and beat until smooth.

Make the almond filling. Mash or grate the almond paste until softened. Add the egg white and sugar and mix until well blended.

Make the egg wash by combining the beaten egg and water in a small bowl.

Heat the oven to 400° F.

Divide the dough into thirds. Roll 1/3 to a 16" x 8" rectangle. Cut into 8 4"-inch squares. Place a scant tablespoon of filling into the center of each and fold opposite corners to the middle brushing with egg wash and pressing to seal. Repeat with remaining dough. (You can also wrap remaining dough tightly and freeze until needed.) Let stand at room temperature 15 minutes.

Brush with egg wash and sprinkle with Swedish pearl sugar. Bake 15 to 20 minutes or until golden brown. Cool on a wire cooling rack.

Baked Apples with Honey and Almonds

Baked apples make a healthy dessert that always reminds me of autumn, especially when the new crop of apples arrive at the farmers' market. Honeycrisp is a relatively new variety that you might want to try. It is sweet and juicy and good for baking. Serve with whipped cream, ice cream or Greek-style yogurt, the healthy choice!

MAKES **6** SERVINGS

3	large baking apples (Gala, Braeburn, Granny Smith)	1/4 cup	firmly packed light brown sugar
1/3 cup	coarsely ground almonds	2 tablespoons	butter, softened
		1/2 cup	orange juice
		2 tablespoons	honey

Heat the oven to 400° F. Cut the apples in half lengthwise and remove the core and stem end. A melon baller works well for this. Place the apples cut side up in a pie pan or shallow baking dish.

Combine the almonds, brown sugar and butter and spoon into the center of each apple. Divide the filling evenly, mounding as needed.

Combine the orange juice and honey in a glass measuring cup and microwave 30 seconds to warm slightly and dissolve the honey. Pour over the apples.

Bake 35 to 45 minutes or until the apples are fork tender and the topping is browned.

Danish Fishing Trawler
Ole Akhøj / Danish Media Center

PRESERVED SALMON AND COD

Salmon preserved by smoking is popular in all the Scandinavian countries. Norwegian salmon is prized throughout the world. Milder than Scottish smoked salmon, Norwegian smoked salmon is prepared over special woods that add a distinctive flavor. Norwegian salmon comes primarily from the crystal waters in Norway and the North Atlantic. Today, much of it is also farmed.

Salmon may be hot- or cold-smoked or cured. Gravlax is made from salmon that is cured in salt, sugar and dill. It's usually served with a mustard dill sauce and brown bread or potatoes.

Lutefisk is eaten in Norway, Sweden, Finland and those parts of the United States and Canada that have large Scandinavian populations. It's made from dried cod treated with lye which gives it its distinctive odor and flavor. The lye acts as a preservative and is soaked out of the fish before cooking. Lutefisk is often served with a white sauce and side dishes such as potatoes, lefse, rutabagas and peas.

Meringue with Peaches and Raspberries

You can also top this fancy dessert with fresh local fruits such as strawberries, rasbperries and blueberries. Fresh peaches have such a short season, I use them whenever I can. Because some peach varieties brown more than others, toss them with a tablespoon of lemon juice after slicing. The almond extract is optional but I like to use it with peaches.

MAKES **6** TO **8** SERVINGS

MERINGUE

1 cup	superfine sugar		1/2 teaspoon	cream of tartar
1 tablespoon	cornstarch		1/2 teaspoon	vanilla
4	large egg whites, room temperature		1/2 teaspoon	almond extract, if desired
2 cups	heavy whipping cream		2	peaches, peeled, sliced and pitted
2 tablespoons	granulated sugar		1 cup	fresh raspberries

Heat the oven to 300° F. Line a baking sheet with parchment paper and draw a 9" circle on the paper by tracing around a 9" cake pan. Place drawing side down on a baking sheet.

Make the meringue. Whisk the sugar and the cornstarch together in a small bowl. Beat the egg whites in a large mixer bowl using the whisk attachment until frothy and beat in the cream of tartar, vanilla and almond extract. Gradually add the sugar mixture, 1 tablespoon at a time, beating on high speed until the sugar is dissolved and the meringue holds stiff glossy peaks when the beater is lifted, 4 to 6 minutes. (To use granulated sugar in place of superfine sugar, place 1 cup + 1 teaspoon granulated sugar in a food processor. Process several seconds until the sugar is finely ground.)

Spoon the meringue into the circle on the parchment and spread to the edge using a metal spatula, mounding slightly higher around the edge. Place in the oven and reduce the heat to 250° F. Bake for 50 to 60 minutes or until firm and dry to the touch. Any cracks may look slightly moist. Remove and cool completely on a wire cooling rack. When cool, carefully peel off the paper. (If the meringue cracks, you can "mend" it with whipped cream or just layer it into bowls and top with whipped cream and fruit.)

Whip the cream on high speed in a large mixer bowl with the whisk attachment until soft peaks form. Add the sugar and continue beating until slightly stiff. Chill until serving.

Just before serving, place the meringue shell on a serving dish. Spread the whipped cream into the center, leaving about 1" around the edge of the meringue. Arrange the fresh fruit on top of the whipped cream. Store any remaining dessert in the refrigerator.

Wooden Boat and Holiday Cabins
Christer Lundin / Stockholm Visitors Board

MAKING A MERINGUE

When making a meringue, it is easier to separate the white from the yolk when the eggs are cold, and it's essential to have no yolk in with the whites. Since eggs beat to the highest volume when they are at room temperature, allow the whites to stand at room temperature about 30 minutes before beating. Gradually add the cream of tartar to stabilize the foam. After very soft peaks form, begin adding the sugar. Once you begin adding sugar, you are less likely to overbeat because it stabilizes the whites. Continue beating until the sugar dissolves. You can test this by rubbing a little meringue between your fingers to see if you can feel the sugar crystals. The meringue will form stiff glossy peaks that do not fall when properly beaten. Don't prepare a meringue on a humid day or drops of moisture will appear on the surface after baking.

Swedish Kringle

After you have made this delectable dessert, you will be able to make cream puffs or éclairs because the basic pastry is the same. The eggy paste will puff up late in the baking and fall when it is removed from the oven, making an inner layer like custard. The sweet frosting flows into the nooks and crannies of the pastry, and adds a sweet finish.

MAKES **2, 10** SERVINGS EACH

CRUST

1 cup	all-purpose flour		1 tablespoon	water
1/2 cup	cold unsalted butter			

TOPPING

1 cup	water		3	large eggs, room temperature
1/2 cup	unsalted butter			
1 cup	all-purpose flour		1 teaspoon	almond extract

FROSTING

2 cups	confectioners' sugar		3 tablespoons	heavy whipping cream or whole milk
1 tablespoon	butter, softened			
1 teaspoon	almond extract			

Heat the oven to 350° F. Make the crust. Place the flour and butter in the bowl of a food processor. Pulse until mixture resembles coarse crumbs with some pea-sized pieces. With the machine running, add the water and process until a dough is formed. Put dough on a lightly floured surface and shape into a ball. Divide the dough in half. Press each half into a strip about 3" wide and 10" long on an ungreased baking sheet.

Make the topping. Heat the water and butter in a medium saucepan over medium-high heat until the butter is melted and the liquid is boiling. Add the flour all at once and whisk until a thick paste forms and leaves the sides of the pan. Cook about 1 minute longer, stirring constantly to evaporate excess moisture. Remove from the heat and cool at least 5 minutes to prevent the eggs from cooking when you add them.

Using a hand mixer or whisk, beat in the eggs, one at a time, beating well after each egg. Each egg should be completely mixed in before the next egg is added. Stir in the almond extract.

Spread over the pastry strips, spreading almost to the edges. Bake 50 to 60 minutes or until puffed and golden brown. Cool on wire cooling rack. As the pastry cools, it will collapse. Cool completely.

Make the frosting. Mix the confectioners' sugar, butter, almond extract and 2 tablespoons whipping cream until smooth. Add more whipping cream if needed for spreading consistency. Spread over pastry and cut into slices before serving.

Sailboat Regatta in Stockholm
Christer Lundin / Stockholm Visitors Board

PATE A CHOUX

Pate a choux or choux paste is the dough used to make cream puffs and éclairs. It should be smooth and shiny, very thick and slightly sticky. Cooling the hot paste before adding the eggs is essential so that the eggs do not cook when they are added as they provide the leavening in baking. Add the flour all at once and stir constantly until thickened. Some of the butter may separate but this is just because the water is evaporating. Because the dough is thick, it can be piped with a pastry bag or simply shaped.

For cream puffs, the baked pastry is pierced to dry the inside somewhat but for Swedish Kringle, it collapses and forms an inner custard-like layer.

SCANDINAVIAN TRADITIONAL FAVORITES

WHEN PEOPLE IMMIGRATE to a new country they are often seeking prosperity, easier lives or basic freedoms. They bring their native traditions to their new country as a way to stay connected to their native lands.

Lefse is an essential part of any celebration when Norwegians gather. For best results, a special rolling pin with grooves aids in rolling it very thin and lefse sticks make it easier to turn. A potato ricer is essential for the best texture.

Lingonberry jam is popular in Sweden because lingonberries grow wild on a tree-like shrub in areas with a cool climate. They are easily harvested by anyone willing to pick and clean the berries.

Many foods are associated with the holidays. Fattigmann, a Norwegian Christmas day favorite, need to be prepared at home and cutting is easier with a special utensil but not necessary. Sandbakkels, baked in tiny tins, can be served plain or with decadent fillings. The secret to making Spritz is having the dough at the right consistency so that it adheres to the baking sheet when pressed out. You can use different shapes, colors and decorations but in many Swedish homes, spritz cookies are shaped like an "S." Many Danish families serve Aebleskiver on Christmas Eve or the next morning.

Stockholm Harbor at Christmas
Henrik Trygg / Stockholm Visitors Board

Danish Aebleskiver

To prepare these Danish pancake balls you need a special pan with 7 rounded cups (see Sources, page 96). Most aebleskiver pans are made of cast iron or heavy cast aluminum. Traditionally a knitting needle is used to turn the balls as they cook and I find it easiest. You can also use a wooden skewer. The secret to round balls is to turn several times before the batter is completely cooked.

Makes 35 pancake balls

4	large eggs, separated		2 cups	2% milk
2 tablespoons	sugar		1/4 cup	butter, softened
2 cups	all-purpose flour			Confectioners' sugar
1 teaspoon	baking powder			Applesauce, if desired
1/2 teaspoon	salt			

Whisk the egg yolks and sugar until foamy. Combine the flour, baking powder and salt in a medium bowl. Add the flour and milk to the egg yolks and whisk until smooth.

Beat the egg whites in a large bowl with the electric mixer on high speed until soft peaks form. When you lift the beaters, the whites will make peaks that fold back slightly.

Gently fold the egg whites into the batter until smooth (see *How to Fold*, page 39).

Heat an aebleskiver pan over medium heat until drops of water sizzle. Place about 1/4 teaspoon butter in each cup. Add about 1/4 cup batter to each cup. Each cup should be about 3/4 full. Cook 1 to 2 minutes or until bottom half is browned. Use the knitting needle to slowly turn balls to cook the other sides. Balls are done when a wooden pick inserted in the center comes out clean.

Turn out pancake balls onto plate and keep warm in a slow oven. Dust with confectioners' sugar and serve with applesauce.

Frigate St. George in Tivoli Gardens
SØren Lauridsen / Denmark Media Center

Tivoli Gardens

Tivoli Gardens, opened in 1843 just outside of Copenhagen, is the second oldest amusement park in the world and inspired Walt Disney's creation of Disneyland. In the 1850s, the city expanded and today Tivoli sits in the heart of Copenhagen. The park is known for its wooden roller coaster, one of the world's oldest still in operation. The Pantomime Theater is an open-air theater built in the Chinese style where Columbine and Harlequin still perform. It is the oldest building at Tivoli and famous for its peacock curtain.

In the summer the fairy tale gardens are filled with thousands of flowers and are a popular place for locals and tourists. At night the sky is lit with over 100,000 lights. During the Christmas season even more lights shine. The small villages are filled with lights and over 70 different stall keepers showcase holidays gifts and décor.

Swedish Pepparkakor

Traditional shapes for these spicy cookies include pigs, horses, roosters, gingerbread boys, hearts and stars. The most common shape in Sweden is the pig! Many families hang Pepperkakor as ornaments on Christmas trees along with small animals made from straw.

MAKES **6** DOZEN COOKIES

3 1/2 cups	all-purpose flour		1 cup	sugar
2 teaspoons	baking soda		1/2 cup	firmly packed
2 teaspoons	cinnamon			light brown sugar
1 1/2 teaspoons	ground ginger		1 cup	butter, softened
1/2 teaspoon	salt		1	large egg, beaten
1/2 teaspoon	ground cloves		2 tablespoons	dark molasses

Combine the flour, baking soda, cinnamon, ground ginger, salt and ground cloves in a medium bowl. Whisk until spices are thoroughly mixed into flour.

Beat the sugar, brown sugar and butter in a large mixer bowl with an electric mixer on medium speed until creamy. Add the egg and molasses and beat on medium until well mixed.

With the mixer on low speed, add the flour mixture. Beat until a soft dough is formed.

Shape the dough into a ball and divide in half. Wrap in waxed paper and chill at least 2 hours.

Heat the oven to 375° F.

Remove half of dough from the refrigerator and place on a well-floured surface. Roll out to 1/8" thickness. Cut into shapes with cookie cutters and place on baking sheets.

(For cut-out cookies, I like to use a pastry cloth and a rolling pin with a cover. Experiment to discover what is easiest for you.)

Bake 7 to 9 minutes or until the edges begin to brown. Cool on wire cooling racks. Repeat with the remaining dough.

Decorate as desired.

Christmas Market at Tivoli
Dorte Krogh / Denmark Media Center

DALA HORSE

The tradition of carving wood scraps into horses began about 400 years ago in central Sweden in the province of Dalarna. Legend has it that the horses were carved in the long evening hours by woodcutters far from home when the weather prevented outdoor work or by furniture makers who used scraps they carried home. When Sweden was at war in the 1700s, soldiers quartered in the homes of citizens carved the horses and used them to trade for food.

Today the Dala horses are made of pine, which is dried for three to four weeks before carving so that the wood doesn't split. The classic red color comes from the copper mines located nearby. The flowered saddle pattern comes from the Bible story of the kurbit, or gourd vine, that grew around Jonah outside the city of Ninevah and protected him from the desert sun.

The horses are painted by talented artisans in many colors and styles that are related to different regions. Sometimes as many as nine artisans are involved in making one Dala Horse.

Fattigman

Traditional Norwegian cookies, Fattigman are "poor man's cakes" named for the original country bakers who created the recipe. This recipe came from a friend who anticipated her mom frying them every Christmas Day. You can buy a fattigmann cutter (see Sources, page 96) but they can easily be shaped by following the directions below.

MAKES 3 DOZEN COOKIES

3	large eggs	3 1/2 cups	all-purpose flour
3/4 cup	sugar	1/4 teaspoon	salt
1/4 cup	heavy whipping ceam	Vegetable oil for deep fat frying	
1/4 cup	butter, melted	Confectioners' sugar	
1 1/2 teaspoons	vanilla		

Place the eggs in a large mixer bowl and beat until foamy with the whisk attachment. Gradually beat in the sugar on low speed. Increase the speed to high and beat until thick and lemon colored, about 3 minutes.

Reduce the mixer speed to low and add the whipping cream, butter and vanilla. Gradually beat in the flour and salt and mix until a soft dough is formed.

Wrap the dough in waxed paper and chill several hours or overnight.

Heat the oil in a deep fat fryer or heavy saucepan to 375° F. Divide the dough in half and place half on a well-floured surface. Roll dough to 3/8" thickness and cut into 1" strips. Create diamond shapes by cutting strips diagonally every 2 1/2".

Cut a 1" slit between two corners and pull the opposite corner through to the other side. Fry the dough in hot oil until golden brown, about 1 to 2 minutes, turning once. Drain on paper towels. Sprinkle with confectioners' sugar.

Winter Cabin with Holiday Lights
Thomas Skyum / Innovation Norway

SCANDINAVIAN CHRISTMAS

The Christmas season in Scandinavia is the most eagerly awaited time of the year. The long dark, cold nights are brightened with candles, Christmas lights and traditions. For some it begins the first Sunday of Advent and doesn't end until St. Knut's Day, January 13th. In Sweden the season begins December 13th, St. Lucia's Day, when the eldest daughter portrays St. Lucia and serves her parents St. Lucia Buns in bed.

A mischievous elf, Nisse (usually Norwegian) and a tomte (usually Swedish), plays pranks on people. Because he is a good elf, many families leave him a bowl of rice pudding or porridge so his jokes don't get out of hand. On Christmas Eve he leaves gifts for all, and families dance around gaily decorated Christmas trees brightened with red and white hearts, straw ornaments and lights or candles. In all Scandinavian countries, hundreds of cookies are baked so no guest will find hospitality lacking.

Norwegian Lefse

2 1/2 to 3 pounds	russet potatoes, peeled and quartered		4 teaspoons	sugar
1/2 cup	heavy whipping cream		1 teaspoon	salt
1/2 cup	butter		2 cups	all-purpose flour

Cook potatoes in salted water until tender. Drain well. Press warm potatoes through a ricer into a large mixing bowl. Measure 5 cups riced potatoes. Add whipping cream, butter, sugar and salt. Mix well. Cool completely and refrigerate over night.

Divide potatoes in half. Stir in 1 cup flour into 1/2 of the potatoes. Place on a lightly floured surface and knead gently to form a dough. Divide into 9 pieces and roll into balls.

On a lightly-floured pastry cloth and using a stockinet-covered rolling pin, roll each ball as thin as possible to an 8" to 9" circle.

Heat an electric griddle to 400° F. Using a large inset spatula or lefse stick place lefse on griddle. Cook about 2 minutes or until browned. Gently flip over and cook 1 to 2 minutes or until second side is browned. Remove from griddle and place on a clean towel. Use waxed paper between lefse.

Repeat with the second half of the potatoes, adding the remaining cup of flour. Cooked lefse can be refrigerated for 2 days. For longer storage, wrap tightly and freeze.

Serve with butter and cinnamon sugar.

Swedish Pancakes with Lingonberries

1 1/2 cups	all-purpose flour		1/4 teaspoon	salt
2 cups	2% milk		3 tablespoons	butter, melted and cooled
5	large eggs, beaten		Lingonberry jam	
1/3 cup	sugar			

Combine the flour, milk, eggs, sugar and salt in a large mixing bowl. Beat until the batter is smooth. Stir in the butter. Cover and let stand at room temperature about 20 to 30 minutes.

Heat a 9" nonstick skillet until drops of water sizzle. Add about 1/3 cup pancake batter to the bottom of the pan. Rotate the pan until the bottom is evenly covered. Cook 1 to 2 minutes or until the bottom of the pancake is lightly browned. Adjust the heat as needed.

Using a rubber spatula, lift the pancake and turn to cook the second side. Cook until browned, about 1 to 2 minutes.

Roll or fold pancake and keep warm in a low oven. Serve pancakes with lingonberry jam. Other accompaniments include whipped cream, maple syrup or other flavors of jam.

Sandbakkels

MAKES ABOUT **5** DOZEN COOKIES

1/2 cup	unsalted butter, softened	1	large egg
1/2 cup	vegetable shortening	1 teaspoon	almond extract
1 cup	sugar	2 1/2 cups	all-purpose flour

Heat the oven to 375° F. Spray sandbakkel tins (see *Sources*, page 96) with nonstick cooking spray.

Beat the butter and shortening in a large mixer bowl with electric mixer on medium speed until creamy. Add sugar gradually and beat until well mixed. Beat in the egg and almond extract and mix well.

With the mixer on low speed add the flour and continue beating until dough forms.

Using about 1 teaspoon of dough, press into individual sandbakkel tins. Do not extend above the rim or it will be harder to remove the cookie after baking. The amount of dough in each tin will vary depending on the size of the tin. This will also affect the final yield. Place the prepared tins on a baking sheet. (If the dough is too soft to handle, chill about 1/2 hour.)

Bake cookies 12 to 15 minutes or until edges are lightly browned.

Let cookies cool on a wire cooling rack about 10 minutes. To remove cookies, press sides of tins to loosen. Remove and cool completely.

Dust with confectioners' sugar if you aren't filling them. Sandbakkels can be filled with whipped cream, jam or jelly, lemon curd or chocolate ganache.

Swedish Spritz

MAKES **6** TO **7** DOZEN COOKIES

1 cup	unsalted butter, softened	2 1/2 cups	all-purpose flour
1 cup	confectioners' sugar	1/4 teaspoon	salt
1	large egg		Food colors
1 teaspoon	almond extract		Colored sugar, if desired

Heat the oven to 400° F.

Combine the flour and salt in a small bowl.

Beat the sugar and butter in a large mixer bowl with electric mixer on medium speed until creamy. Beat in the egg and almond extract and beat until well mixed.

With the mixer on low speed add the flour mixture. Beat until a soft dough is formed.

Divide the dough into 3 or 4 parts and color as desired. Place one part dough in a cookie press and form cookies on ungreased baking sheets about 1" apart. Chill remaining dough until needed.

Bake cookies 7 to 9 minutes or until edges just begin to brown. Cool on baking sheet 1 minute and remove. Cool completely on a wire cooling rack.

INDEX

The Islet of Riddarholmen
Alexander Dokukin / Stockholm Visitors Board

ACKNOWLEDGMENTS

Many people, family and friends, helped make this cookbook a reality and to them I offer my gratitude and love. My husband, Duncan, who didn't expect to spend his summer selecting photos, encouraged me in every way and made it possible for us to meet our deadline. My family tested recipes when I was in a crunch and cheered me on.

Many friends who offered advice and support and tested recipes, especially my friends the Reynolds, who returned from Scandinavia with photos of food and props for my photo shoot. And to those friends who offered treasured family recipes and the stories behind the recipes, thank you very much.

I also want to thank:

My photographer, Joel Butkowski, who created beautiful shots and encouraged my food styling efforts.

Food stylist, Ann Jensen, who added her special touch to many of the food photos and generously shared her props.

Beth Farrell whose design talent and calm helped in more ways than she knows.

My agents, Gordon Warnock and Andrea Hurst, who are always working for me.

And Pelican Books for giving me the opportunity to create this *Scandinavian Classic*.

SOURCES

Ingrebretsen's Scandinavian Gifts (1-800-279-9333)
www.Ingebretsens.com

Wilton Industries (1-800-794-5866)
www.wilton.com

Williams-Sonoma (1-800-541-2233)
www.Williams-Sonoma.com